Allan and Barbara Pease are the most successful relationship authors in the business. They have written a total of 15 bestsellers including 9 number ones – and give seminars in up to 30 countries each year. Their books are available in over 100 countries, are translated into 51 languages and have sold over 25 million copies. They appear regularly in the media worldwide and their work has been the subject of 9 television series, a stage play and a No. 1 box office movie which attracted a combined audience of over 100 million.

Their company, Pease International Ltd, produces videos, training courses and seminars for business and governments worldwide. Their monthly relationship column was read by over 20 million people in 25 countries. They have 6 children and 5 grandkids and are based in Australia and the UK.

Their bestsellers include: *Why Men Don't Listen & Women Can't Read Maps*, *The Definitive Book of Body Language*, *Why Men Don't Have a Clue & Women Always Need More Shoes*, *Easy Peasey: People Skills for Life* and *Questions are the Answers*.

By Allan & Barbara Pease

WHY HE'S SO LAST MINUTE AND SHE'S
GOT IT ALL WRAPPED UP

THE DEFINITIVE BOOK OF BODY LANGUAGE

WHY MEN DON'T HAVE A CLUE AND
WOMEN ALWAYS NEED MORE SHOES

WHY MEN DON'T LISTEN AND
WOMEN CAN'T READ MAPS

QUESTIONS ARE THE ANSWERS

TALK LANGUAGE

WHY MEN CAN ONLY DO ONE THING AT A TIME
AND WOMEN NEVER STOP TALKING

THE MATING GAME: WHY MEN WANT SEX AND
WOMEN NEED LOVE

BODY LANGUAGE IN THE WORK PLACE
THE BODY LANGUAGE OF LOVE

The Mating Game

WHY MEN WANT SEX
& WOMEN NEED LOVE

Allan & Barbara Pease

An Orion paperback

First published in Great Britain in 2009
as Why Men Want Sex & Women Need Love:
Unravelling the Simple Truth
by Orion Books
This paperback edition published in 2010
by Orion,
an imprint of Orion Books Ltd,
Orion House, 5 Upper St Martin's Lane,
London WC2H 9EA

An Hachette UK company

3 5 7 9 10 8 6 4

Published by arrangement with PEASE INTERNATIONAL PTY LTD

Copyright © Allan Pease 2009

A CIP catalogue record for this book
is available from the British Library.

ISBN 978-1-4091-0239-7

Printed and bound by CPI Group (UK) Ltd, Croydon, CR0 4YY

The Orion Publishing Group's policy is to use papers that
are natural, renewable and recyclable products and
made from wood grown in sustainable forests. The logging
and manufacturing processes are expected to conform to
the environmental regulations of the country of origin.

Every effort has been made to fulfil requirements with regard to
reproducing copyright material. The author and publisher will be
glad to rectify any omissions at the earliest opportunity

www.orionbooks.co.uk

Why not use Allan Pease as guest speaker for your next conference or seminar?

Allan and Barbara Pease are the most successful relationship authors in the business. They have written a total of 15 bestsellers - Including 9 number ones - and give seminars in up to 30 countries each year. Their books are available in over 100 countries, are translated into 51 languages and have sold over 25 million copies. They appear regularly in the media worldwide and their work has been the subject of 9 television series, a stage play and a number one box office movie which attracted a combined audience of over 100 million.

Their company, Pease International Ltd, produces videos, training courses and seminars for business and governments worldwide. Their monthly relationship column was read by over 20 million people in 25 countries. They have 6 children and 5 grandkids and are based in Australia and the UK.

Acknowledgements

Thank you to those who contributed to this book, whether they knew it or not:

Kelly Bradtke, Andrew and Joanne Parish, Decima McAuley, Rebecca Schell, Melissa Stewart, Jasmine Pease, Cameron Pease, Brandon Pease, Bella Pease, Michael Pease, Adam Sellars, John MacIntosh, Norman Leonard, Ken Wright, Amanda Gore, Daniel Clarke, Dr Janet Hall, Col and Jill Haste, Kirsty and Scott Gooderham, Phil Gray, Shirley Neale and Danny Redman, Des Wilmore, Bernie de Souza, Dr James Moir, Helen and Ian Belcher, Roger Loughnan, Ivanna Fugalot, Dr Gennady Polonsky, Christine Walding, Jeff Turner, John Lanesmith, Sally Berghofer, Rob and Sue Keam, Dave Stewart, David C. Smith, Dr John Tickel, Professor Graeme Jackson, Nicole Kilpatrick, Josephine and Rick, Glen Fraser, Tony Rich, Dr Michael Walsh, Angus Woodhead, Fiona Hedger, Gary Crick, Anthony Gorman, Brian Tracy, Jenny Cooper, Ivor Ashfield, Trevor Velt, Jo Abbott, Alan Holliday, Graeme Shiels, Shorty Tully, Kerri-Anne Kennerley, Sue Williams, Janine Good, Bert Newton, Graham Smith, Kevin Fraser, Dr Phillip Stricker, Emma and Graham Steele and Glenda Leonard.

And special thanks to
Dorie Simmonds
and
Ray and Ruth Pease.

Contents

Introduction

*Sue was furious. Admittedly, she had asked them for
a male baby with dark features, a strong nose and
movie-star looks, but this was ridiculous.*

Today we are confronted with sexual situations and circumstances that our ancestors never encountered. We can alter our fertility with hormones, artificial insemination and IVF; we can meet new partners through dating agencies and the Internet; we can improve our appearance with cosmetics or surgery; and we can create new life in a dish. No other species can do any of these things.

As humans, we are experts at studying the mating behaviours of other species. We can predict their actions, even modify them, and we can genetically alter them to change their appearance. When it comes to choosing a mate for ourselves, however, few humans seem to have much success, let alone any real understanding of the process through which it happens. Most animal species seem to have little problem when choosing mates and dealing with relationships. For them, the female goes on heat, the male mates with her, and it's all over.

Humans are the only species that are confused about the mating game.

The state of our relationships with our partners – or our lack of partners – is a constant source of human discussion and one of the prime topics of female conversation everywhere. Few things can give us such joy and elation yet, at the same time, can produce so much pain and despair. Love has always been the most common theme in music, soap operas, romance books, literature, movies and poetry. People in every culture experience love, and every culture has words to describe it.

So what is love? It's a question that has been asked for thousands of years. Researchers from almost all disciplines have tried to discover the nature of love and to convince others of their findings, but none of the answers ever proposed are conclusive. Because of its elusiveness, love constantly calls for definitions and interpretation.

Why do we even have sex? What drives men to constantly search for sex? What compels women to demand commitment from men? We will answer many of these questions in this book. We will show you why sex, love and romance began, reveal the science that says where love sits in the brain and, importantly, tell you what to do about it all. We have used scientific studies, surveys, case studies and humour to make it easy to remember.

Looking for 'the One'

Most of us are raised with the belief that one day we will find 'the One' – that special person with whom we are meant to spend eternity. For the majority of people, however, real life fails to live up to that expectation. Most people who get married believe that it will be 'till death do us part', but divorce rates in many countries are now in excess of 50%, and the rate of extramarital affairs is estimated to be 30–60%, with women being in the lower range and men in the top range.

Divorce rates among those who have lived together and then married range from 25%, in Canada and Spain, to over 50%, in Sweden, Norway and France.

The failure to make a relationship work is seen as a personal failure by most people and sends millions of us to therapists, but conflict in relationships is the norm for almost all species, including humans.

Sex is like air: it's not important unless you aren't getting any.

In the 1980s, it was generally believed that much of human behaviour was learned and could be changed, but we now know that most of it is hardwired into us. In fact, since the end of the 20th century, researchers studying human behaviour have uncovered a mountain of scientific knowledge to demonstrate that we are born with circuitry hardwired into the brain that influences how we act. We also know that cultural factors and myriad environmental forces, such as our teachers, friends, parents and employers, influence how we may think or act. The result is that nature and nurture are inextricably entwined. Imagine that your brain has an operating system like a computer. You're born with it and it has default positions that it retreats to when it's under stress – that's the nature part of us. The nurture part is our environment, and our environment is the software that runs on our hardware.

Nature = our brain's hardware
Nurture = our environment

This is not to say that we are all at the mercy of our DNA. The human brain developed frontal lobes to allow us to choose our actions, but it is important to understand that we come with baggage from our ancestral past. The development of the cerebral cortex – the bit of the brain that collates information from all of the sensory organs, holds memory and thought processes – has allowed us to think, to make choices and to rise above our inherited nature in most things. When it comes to sex, love and romance, however, our ancient hardwiring still compels us to have the same preferences and choices our ancestors did. And, as you will see, there's no escaping it. Your brain has an operating system with default positions. If your computer is stressed or crashes, it operates from its built-in defaults – and so does your brain. The artificial environment of so-called 'equality' that we have created, in which we are expected to pretend to each other that we all desire the same things, is nothing more than politically correct software.

As men and women, we still want different things from sex and love – not better or worse, *different* – and these are largely dictated by our hardware. We can make conscious choices about what we think we want, but our hardwiring will still urge us to go where it wants us to go.

This book will show you how women are just as interested in sex as men are – or 'making love', as women describe it – and will explain how men's and women's sexual urges are triggered by different circumstances, conditions and priorities. We'll examine what men and women really want and will look at casual sex and affairs, and reveal things about sex and love that most people don't know. We'll also give you strategies to increase your market value in the mating game.

> **What's 'making love'?**
> **It's what a woman does**
> **while a man is bonking her.**

How the Western World Got So Screwed Up About Sex

Much of the Western world's current hang-ups about sex can be accredited to Britain's Queen Victoria and her husband, Albert. Victoria's reign, between 1837 and 1901, was characterised by strict moral values, sexual repression and low tolerance of crime. The existence of female homosexuality was denied, while male homosexuality was illegal. Thanks to the British Empire, Victorian values were spread around the world.

At the height of the Victorian era, it was common to conceal furniture legs, such as pianos and tables, in order to prevent sexual arousal. Bathing suits at the time covered almost the entire bodies of both men and women. Victoria even decreed that in polite society a chicken breast was to be called a 'bosom', and she banned advertisements that revealed ladies' underwear. Then, as now, much of society considered nudity and sexual arousal to be synonymous.

**Victorian prudery deemed it improper to
say 'leg' in mixed company; instead,
the word 'limb' was preferred.**

Victorian women were taught never to invite sexual advances or give in to fantasies, and to live in quiet devotion to husband, family and country. A man's social success was based partly on his wife's passiveness, and it was assumed that a woman had no sexual needs of her own. Popular wisdom of the time was that women didn't like sex, and that male sex drive compelled women into 'giving in'. Books available at the time suggested that a decent husband wouldn't expect sex from his wife more than about once every six months and advised men on things to do to suppress their urge for sex more frequently. In essence, the popular advice to women of the day was to lie back, close your eyes and 'think of England'.

**How does an Englishman know his
wife has died?
Sex is still the same but the
dishes are piling up in the sink.**

It's likely your grandparents or great-grandparents were born in this era and that some of these Victorian attitudes were handed down to you from your parents, whether you realise it or not. If you ever feel awkward when sex is mentioned, or feel embarrassed by sexual jokes and try to change the subject, you can probably attribute your discomfort to the influence of Victorian values. This is why English-speaking countries, especially Britain, have so many more sexual hang-ups compared to those European countries who *weren't* influenced by Victorian morals. If you have no cultural connection to the Victorian era but still feel awkward when discussing any aspect of sex and sexuality, then you'll probably be able to trace these attitudes back to religion or to leaders who exerted power by insisting that their followers adhere to their own twisted sense of morality.

The Statistics

Today, there is a 50% chance a marriage will fail and about an 85% chance the wife will be the instigator. It is estimated that every day in the UK alone three men who are facing crippling child-support payments commit suicide. The system works on the principle that the more you earn, the more you pay. These men feel it's impossible to get ahead and get their lives back. Being in a relationship and having children can make your life wonderful, but when a relationship ends badly, it can make you ill or even suicidal. This is why it is so important to understand how your brain chooses your partners for you.

In Europe, for every marriage there is now one divorce. This means fewer people are getting married and past marriages are ending. Around 30% of all second marriages also end in divorce.

This book is based on current research and not on folklore, myths, the stars, romantic notions or politically correct ideals. Most of what we will discuss is evidence-based. We have drawn from a wide array of research, ranging from empirical studies and scientific experiments to relationship surveys from many sources, including our own, and from other data collected about why we behave as we do or why we think the things we think. If what we analysed did not have some scientific or credible evidence base, we disregarded it. Most of the research data we refer to is listed in the back of the book.

During the six years it took to write and research this book, we (the middle-aged authors) gave birth to two children through IVF, dealt with prostate cancer and all its downsides, and encountered many of the obstacles that can stifle or end any couple's love life, so we will be drawing here not only on research but also on our own personal experiences, observations and strategies, as well as those of others we met on this journey.

Enjoy!

Allan and Barbara Pease

Chapter 1
Sex On the Brain

It says, 'Then insert tab A into slot B.'

Passion, infatuation, romance, 'the hots', obsessive love, beer goggles...these are the words we use to describe those feelings of ecstasy, elation, bliss and rapture that almost every person will experience in some way at some time in their lives. With them come the feelings of anguish, distress, pain, agony, torment and grief. For thousands of years, experts have tried, with little success, to define romantic love, usually concluding that it must be controlled somehow by forces outside ourselves, such as the mystical, supernatural or spiritual. Yet we have no difficulty in pigeon-holing other human emotions, like depression, anxiety, obsession and fear.

Since the 1970s, humans have experienced a deep spiritual yearning for love. This yearning is caused by the breakdown of the social structures that gave us intimate connections with friends, family and lovers, and was the norm for thousands of years. We evolved as a species that cared for our young, protected, loved and depended on each other, and stuck together as social and family units. The older generations cared for the children, while the middle generation worked or collected food. In the evenings, the older generations told children stories and taught them about their heritage and about life. This kind of family structure now only exists in primitive cultures, parts of the Middle-East, Asia, the Mediterranean and in Third World cultures. And as more and more people are staying single or living alone, this cultural chasm continues to widen. For a million years or more, societies have been structured to bring men and women together; today's societies, however, are driving them apart. The erosion of the basic family structure has led to loss of values, kids growing up without fathers, and emotional chaos.

Same Goals, Different Agendas

Men and women have very different agendas when it comes to sex and love, and these are deeply embedded in our ancient

Victims of love gone wrong fill the depression and suicide clinics everywhere.

past. In basic terms, today's men are turned on by visual images and by the signs of a woman's health, fertility and youth, while women are turned on by the markers of a man's power, status, commitment and material resources – just like their ancestors were. In fact, nothing much has really changed for hundreds of thousands of years in terms of our sexual urges and drives. This can be an unpopular idea in a politically correct world in which it has become fashionable to say that men and women want the same things in life and have the same motivations, preferences and urges, but as you read on, you will see that this is simply not true. In fact, deep down you *know* it's not. This myth is perpetuated by power-seekers, such as bureaucrats, Church leaders, feminist groups and other politically motivated individuals. It may be politically correct to say that men and women think the same way and want the same things, but if you have had any experience living with them, working with them or managing them, you'll know that it isn't true.

The Power of Love

David Buss, professor of psychology at the University of Texas at Austin, is internationally recognised for his evolutionary research on human sex differences in mate selection. He and his team searched for evidence of romantic love in 147 cultures. They discovered empirical proof of romantic love in cave drawings, manuscripts, poems, songs and books. Most people see only the positive sides of love when they think about it – they imagine staring into a lover's eyes, holding hands, singing love songs, making love and warm, fuzzy feelings, all the 'happily-ever-after' stuff – but love also has a dark side. Buss and other researchers found evidence spread throughout human history of love potions, love charms, love spells, suicide and murder motivated by love won or lost. In fact, one in four murders is the result of love gone wrong. Spouses, lovers, rivals, stalkers and jilted lovers everywhere die as a result. Almost every culture has its equivalent of the Romeo and Juliet story. The dramatic urge to love fills us with exhilaration, despair, fear or revenge, often all at the same time.

**Love is about chemical
reactions in the brain.**

And because romantic love is universal and every human culture on earth has it, there must be a biological basis for it. In other words, it can't simply be a cultural tradition, like idol worship or religion; love is something that is very powerful and is hardwired into each of us.

The Biology of Love

Scientists who have been researching how the human brain operates when a person is in love have concluded that there are three distinct brain systems for mating and reproduction – lust, romantic love and long-term attachment.

Each of these systems is associated with distinct hormone activity that cause specific feelings and behavioural changes in lovers. When you think of love in terms of these three systems, it makes it easier to follow what stage a person is in and to better understand their actions.

The purpose of this chapter is to help you understand the basic brain functions that govern lust, romantic love and long-term attachment. We have attempted to keep the explanations as brief and simple as possible. Where we talk about specific areas of the brain it's important to understand that the brain regions discussed are usually part of an overall brain network, and we thank Professor Graeme Jackson of the Brain Research Institute in Melbourne for his suggestions in this area. We have simplified things here to make them more accessible to our readers; at the same time, we are conscious of not oversimplifying these ideas and concepts. It is vital to have this knowledge of the research because it's referred to throughout this book. We use medical terminology for the technically inclined, but you will only need to understand its significance in relation to your love life. We will be discussing principles that operate most of the time for most people, not how minorities or the exceptions behave.

Love has been shown to be the result of a specific group of chemicals and brain circuits working in specific areas of the brain. In simple scientific terms, love is triggered by a combination of brain chemicals, including dopamine, oxytocin, testosterone, oestrogen and norepinephrine; in much the same way, these chemicals drive other mammals to find suitable partners. Once our brain has identified a suitable partner based on certain criteria, which are discussed later, the brain goes into overdrive to produce the chemicals necessary to create the environment to attract that person.

Throughout human history, marriages were an arranged event based on wealth, status, family rivalries, tribal groups and politics. Today, this approach has generally disappeared from the Western world and most people now marry for love.

When it comes to mate selection, humans focus their attention on just one person. This distinguishes them from most other animals. A courting male pigeon, for example, will puff up his feathers and approach as many potential partners as his energy will allow. Humans, however, usually have a shortlist of candidates but intensely target just one.

Love At First Sight

The phenomenon of 'love at first sight' has been scientifically proven and affects most animal species in much the same way.

Ray was shopping in the supermarket when he glanced between the cornflake packets into the confectionery aisle. What he saw overwhelmed him and he experienced a euphoric feeling, almost as if he was intoxicated. Standing there was a woman who simply captured his heart. She was not beautiful in the usual sense, but there was something unique about her and the way she moved. All he knew was that he felt magnetically drawn to her. Just looking at her filled him with excitement and gave him butterflies in his stomach.

While he experienced these feelings of elation at discovering her, however, he had at the same time a sense of despair because he would never have her.

If you've ever experienced love at first sight, your brain was producing huge amounts of the chemicals dopamine and nor-epinephrine, which make you feel almost as if you are on drugs. The same things happen to other animals. Take, for example, the female prairie vole, which is similar to a desert rat. If you expose a female prairie vole to even a tiny scent of male vole urine, she experiences exactly the same chemical reaction as humans do: a surge of dopamine and norepineph-rine. One study demonstrated that when female sheep that are on heat are shown images of male sheep, norepinephrine lev-els in their brains surge. While this effect lasts for seconds or minutes for most animals, it can last for months or years in humans.

Scientists now agree that love at first sight is a real phenom-enon. Scientists working in this area also believe that in a stable society in which people are not under the threat of death or war, lust, romantic love and long-term attachment may be the best and most efficient way to ensure species survival.

Darwin Made Me Do It

Lust is brought on by surges in sex hormones, such as testos-terone and oestrogen. These hormones cause an urgent push for physical gratification. During lust, two key parts of the brain become active – the hypothalamus, which controls our primordial drives, such as thirst and hunger, and the amygdale, which is a centre for arousal. Dopamine is heavily secreted during lust and it triggers the production of testosterone, causing sexual attraction to occur. It happens when you first see someone and have an overwhelming urge to 'have' that person.

A study conducted in 2006 at the University of Chicago demonstrated that even during a casual chat with a female stranger testosterone levels shoot up by a third in men, and that the stronger this hormonal reaction, the more dramatic the changes in a man's behaviour. The study also showed testosterone readings in married men and fathers are significantly lower than in single males who are 'playing the field' because the fathers have moved into a nurturing, parental role and have higher oxytocin levels than single men, who are still searching for somewhere to pass on their genes.

Lust obviously evolved to lead to procreation and to ensure the survival of the human species and would have been necessary in extremely difficult survival circumstances when there was no time for romance. Also, human females can only bear one offspring a year, which means that, without lust, the human species could be threatened with extinction – because we are slow reproducers, Mother Nature made us enthusiastic procreators. This is why people in dangerous and threatening situations, such as wartime, can suddenly find themselves lusting after each other, even though they are strangers. If their lives are in danger, they have the immediate urge to pass on their genes.

In summary, lust, love at first sight and the obsessive, goal-driven aspects of early love are behaviours that evolved to speed up mating and provide a better chance for successful human reproduction.

Let's Stick Together

Testosterone is the main hormone responsible for sex drive, and men have 10–20 times more of it than women. This is why male sex drive is strong and so urgent. Testosterone makes men hairier, bigger, stronger, more aggressive and hornier than women. But men have significantly *less* oxytocin than women. Oxytocin, known as the 'cuddle hormone', is released in large quantities in men and women during orgasm. As quickly as a man can get an erection his oxytocin dissipates, which is the reason why after-sex cuddles have great importance to women and limited appeal to men.

A study in 2006 by Rebecca Turner, PhD, professor in the Organizational Psychology Division of Alliant International

University in San Francisco, showed that this hormone is the glue of human emotional bonding. When people are pair-bonding – or 'falling in love', as we call it – oxytocin levels are high. This is the hormone that gives us the warm, fuzzy feeling we have for the person of our desire. Having higher levels of oxytocin than men is a major reason why women fall more deeply in love at the start of a new relationship than men. The more oxytocin they produce, the more nurturing they will be and the deeper they will bond with someone. Just hearing their lover's name, an odour associated with them, fantasising about them or hearing a song connected with them raises oxytocin levels. Expensive outfits, perfect make-up, loads of jewellery and a new sports car cannot disguise a woman's emotional condition. If she feels loved and adored, her hormones push blood into her cheeks, making her 'glow', and she will radiate warmth. If she feels unloved and ignored, however, that's easy to see, too.

**What is the difference between
men and women?
A woman wants one man to satisfy
her every little need.
A man wants every woman to satisfy
his one little need.**

The studies by David Buss showed that when couples are in the falling-in-love phase, men's testosterone levels decrease, while their oxytocin levels rise to make the bonding process quicker. This makes men softer, gentler and more easy-going. At the same time, women's testosterone levels rise with the excitement and confidence they feel at the start of a new relationship. This increased testosterone makes women hornier, giving the couple the illusion that male and female sex drives must be the same. When this 'shagathon' period ends, about three to nine months into a new relationship, their sex drives return to the 'default position', leaving a man with the idea that she's gone off sex and giving her the impression that he's a sex maniac. Many relationships end at this point.

Why Lovers Are So Crazy About Each Other

Josephine, a 33-year-old single mother, had devoted her life to bringing up her children by herself. After six months in her new job, she attended the company's annual Christmas party on a cruise ship in Sydney Harbour. She looked glamorous when she arrived at the docks and received many compliments and admiring gazes from male staff. This boosted her confidence and made her feel beautiful. As the ship cruised around on the moonlit water, she was introduced to Rick, a handsome new male executive from the Melbourne office. As they shook hands, her heart started racing. He was tall, dark, handsome, made her laugh and it seemed as if he was as attracted to her as she was to him. After a magical night of dancing and dining, they talked until the early hours of the morning and spent the entire next day and evening together. For Josephine, it felt as if some kind of magical spell had been cast over her.

Returning home to the kids was wonderful, but her mind was full of thoughts about Rick and their time together. She wondered if he missed her as much as she missed him. Over the next few days she started to lose weight and couldn't eat – all she could do was think of him and the beautiful memories. She began phoning him every hour just to tell him she was thinking of him, and she sent him text messages in the early hours of the morning. She began buying him gifts to show him how much she cared. Her kids started to feel neglected and their behaviour began to change for the worse, but she didn't seem to care. She cancelled her son's dental appointment and used the money to buy a plane ticket to fly to see Rick. She thought, Wasn't it her time to think about her own needs and to have a life as well?

In many ways behavioural changes during romantic love resemble a psychosis, and from a biochemical standpoint, passionate love closely imitates substance abuse. Dr John Marsden, the head of the British National Addiction Centre, found that love is addictive in similar ways to cocaine and speed. He concluded that romantic love is a 'booby trap', intended to drive partners together long enough to bond. Anthropologist Dr Helen Fisher, author of *The Anatomy of Love*, described falling in love as 'a distinct set of chemical events occurring in the brain that have similarities with mental illness'. According to Dr Fisher, exactly the same brain circuits that become active when you take cocaine light up when you're in love, and you experience an intense elation, just like when you're high on drugs. Researchers have also connected romantic love to the signalling pathways that use the hormone dopamine, a chemical messenger closely tied to the state of euphoria, craving and addiction.

I Get a Shiver Down My Backbone

The chemicals released from the brain during new love result in a variety of physical feelings and reactions that around 90% of new lovers report to have experienced. These include sleeplessness, loss of appetite, flushing, exhilaration, awkwardness, euphoria, butterflies in the stomach, fast breathing, dizziness, weak knees, heart palpitations, sweaty palms and stuttering. Many of these reactions are linked to the fear of being rejected by the loved one, so it becomes like an evolutionary double whammy of excitement and fear, both at the same time. New lovers not only feel these emotions, they constantly scan the face of their beloved looking for signs of reciprocation.

Carole King summed up perfectly the chemical reactions we have to falling in love in her 1970 song 'I Feel the Earth Move Under My Feet'. This song describes how she felt hot and cold, lost emotional control, felt her heart start trembling and saw the sky come falling down whenever her beloved was around.

These are also common responses to drug addiction.

Love can be a wonderful rollercoaster ride and it happens unexpectedly for most people. They have little warning and no apparent control over it. The feelings come from the primitive part of the brain known as the cerebral cortex, or grey matter, and overpowers the rational, thinking part, making lovers behave in irrational ways – in the same way that the fight-or-flight response makes a person run when confronted by a lion, as opposed to calmly thinking about an escape plan.

The euphoria of love has inspired artists to produce haunting love songs and melodies, and powerful, touching poetry, but the intensity of love can also drive some of those under its influence to jealousy and paranoia. Recent scientific evidence shows it can even dramatically improve our health, with further studies showing it is capable of curing cancer or other diseases. Love even motivates us to continue to live with people whose behaviour is detrimental to our well-being, as in the case of abusive partners.

I Can't Sleep, I Can't Eat

People in the 'falling-in-love' stage are commonly called 'lovesick'. They say they can't eat, don't sleep properly and show repetitive, compulsive behaviours, such as calling their beloved 20–30 times a day. These behaviours have now been linked to the combination of low levels of serotonin and high levels of oxytocin. Serotonin is the neurotransmitter that gives us heightened feelings of awareness, sensitivity to our surroundings and an overall feeling of well-being.

Depression and eating disorders are also associated with low levels of serotonin and anti-depressant medications aim to raise these levels. Women naturally have around 30% more oxytocin than men and this, combined with lower levels of serotonin, can explain why women are more inclined to become 'crazy' about someone, and even intensely obsessive.

> **'Love is only the dirty trick played on us
> to achieve the continuation of the species.'**
>
> W. Somerset Maugham

In 2007, Serge Brand and his colleagues at the Psychiatric University Clinics in Basel, Switzerland, interviewed 113 subjects, all of whom were aged 17. Of those 65 said they had recently fallen in love. Brand found that the love-struck adolescents slept less, acted compulsively more often and had 'lots of crazy ideas and creative energy'. The 'in-love' teenagers were more likely to engage in risky behaviour, such as reckless driving or bungee-jumping. Brand showed that teenagers in the early stages of intense romantic love did not differ from patients having a hypomanic episode. In other words, it's sometimes difficult to differentiate teenagers in love from people who are commonly thought to be crazy.

**If you've ever said you were 'crazy'
about someone, you were spot-on.**

What Brain Scans Reveal

Brain-imaging techniques such as functional magnetic-resonance imaging (fMRI) and magneto-encephalographic scanning (MEG) have opened up a whole new world of possibilities in understanding humans because they enable researchers to study the working human brain without harming the patient.

The study of love and sex in the brain gained momentum in 2002, after English neurobiologists Andreas Bartels and Semir Zeki of University College London conducted a study of young men and women who said they were in a new relationship and described themselves as 'madly in love'. When shown a picture of their lover, their brain activity pattern was significantly different from when looking at a picture of a close friend. The brain scans showed that romantic attraction activated those areas of the brain with a large concentration of receptors for dopamine. Dopamine, you will recall, is the neurotransmitter that affects pleasure and motivation, and is often called the 'happiness hormone'. High levels of dopamine and norepinephrine are linked to heightened attention, short-term memory, hyperactivity, sleeplessness and goal-orientated behaviour. When couples are first captivated by each other, they often show the signs of surging dopamine: increased energy, less need for sleep or food, focused attention and exquisite delight in the smallest details of their new relationship. Bartels and Zeki compared the MRI brain-scan images they took of people in the different emotional states of sexual arousal, feeling happy and cocaine-induced euphoria, and found them to be almost the same.

Might As Well Face It, You're Addicted to Love

The following brain scans show how being 'madly in love' activates the same areas in the brain as addiction to cocaine.

So whether you are in love or high on drugs, you will feel

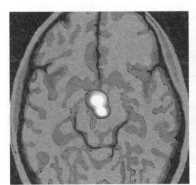 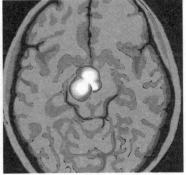

The brain scan on the left shows the region of the brain that is activated in 'crazy-in-love' people. The scan on the right shows the activated regions when using cocaine.

about the same. The scans also revealed that mothers who were looking at their babies had identical brain activity as people who were looking at their lovers. Bartels and Zeki concluded from this that both romantic and maternal love are linked to the perpetuation of the human species, because lovers and babies carry the promise that your DNA will continue.

The Geography of Sex and Love In the Brain

In 2005, Dr Lucy Brown, professor of neuroscience at the Albert Einstein College of Medicine in New York, teamed up with one of the world's most prominent biological anthropologists, Helen Fisher of Rutgers University in the US, and conducted studies with MRI brain scans on 17 young men and women. These were people in a new relationship and described themselves as being 'newly and madly in love' – that is, they were in either the lust or early romantic love stages. Their MRI research explained the physiological reasons behind why we feel what we feel when we fall in love – why love is so powerful and why being rejected is so painful and depressing.

They studied an area in the brain associated with cravings, memory, emotion and attention called the caudate nucleus, and the ventral tegmental – the part of the brain from which dopamine cells are pumped to other areas of the brain. These areas all lit up on the MRI scans as subjects viewed images of their lovers. They also compared the MRI data with the other studies on male penile-erection responses to images of women, and analysed data on both human and animal couples that had been together for a long time. They found that when you fall in love, the ventral tegmental floods the caudate with dopamine. The caudate then sends signals for more dopamine, and the more dopamine you get, the higher and happier you will feel. Fisher and Brown also confirmed that 'crazy love' causes a sensation similar to a substance-induced high because of the hormone activity.

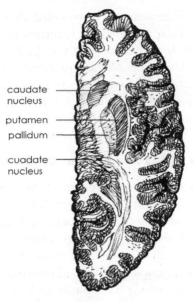

caudate
nucleus

putamen

pallidum

cuadate
nucleus

A cross-section of the human brain

The caudate, they discovered, is the brain area connected with romantic love. They found that long-term attachment was centred in the front and base of the brain in the ventral putamen and the pallidum. Feelings related to lust and sexual arousal occupy different areas, mostly located on the left-hand side of the brain. The important point is that this research removes the mystery of love in the brain and allows us to be more objective about what love really is.

> **Love is a chemical cocktail of happy drugs, and people who are addicted to this cocktail are known as 'sex addicts'.**

Why Men and Women See Love Differently

Fisher and Brown, both separately and together, analysed the brain scans of over 3,000 'madly-in-love' college students, taken while they looked at a picture of their lover. They found that the women in the study showed more activity in the caudate nucleus – as mentioned, an area in the brain associated with memory, emotion and attention – the septum, also called the 'pleasure centre', the posterior parietal cortex, which is involved in the production of mental images, and with memory recall. The men in the study showed more activity in the visual cortex and visual processing areas, including one area responsible for sexual arousal. Bartels and Zeki came to the same conclusions in their study.

The next brain scans illustrate the research carried out by Dr Brown and show where love sits in the brain and why men and women think so very differently about it. These are scans of men and women looking at images of someone they were madly in love with.

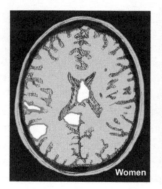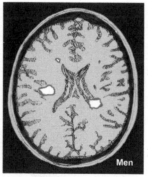

Images of love. Men and women looking at pictures
of their beloved. White areas are active zones.

As you see, men have less lit-up areas than women, but when those areas are viewed in colour, they show men's areas to be more intensely active than women's larger but less active areas. Women not only have more areas being active but they are in completely different locations to men's. This evidence shows why men and women have very different views of love relationships.

Another study showed erotic photos to people as their brains were scanned, but Brown and Fisher found none of the 'in-love' activity areas shown in the above scans. As mentioned earlier, they found activity in the hypothalamus, which controls drives like hunger and thirst, and in the amygdale area, which handles arousal. The bottom line is that brains in love and brains in lust don't look much alike because they each use different systems.

In summary, the science shows entirely different processes are being used to evaluate the opposite sex during early love – men use their eyes as the primary tool to evaluate women for sexual potential, while women use memory to assess a man's characteristics for potential as a long-term partner. Lust and love have different locations in the brain and are *not* the same thing.

How Men's Brains Rate Attractiveness In Women

When Bartels and Zeki showed images of attractive women to men, they found that men showed higher activity in two regions in the brain: one associated with visual stimuli and the other with penile erection (gee, who would have guessed!). The majority of men are highly visual and constantly watch women, fantasise about them and love to look at porn, so this is no surprise to most of us. When these areas in men's brains are lit up, the researchers found that the men's brain areas linked to making moral judgements also diminishes.

> **A three-year-old was examining
> his testicles while taking a bath.
> 'Mom,' he asked, 'are these my brains?'
> 'Not yet,' she replied.**

The visual brain network in men evolved over the last million years because they needed to look at women to size up their ability to produce healthy babies to keep the species going. If a woman was young and healthy, a man would become aroused and start the mating process. This is why men fall in love faster than women – because they are more visually motivated, and visual cues are immediate and send a signal to the brain that activates an instant hormone surge. It also helps to explain why men are more likely than women to fall in love at first sight.

In essence, men use their eyes primarily for evaluating the potential of a woman. When men are turned on, they become flushed with hormones and have erections. These hormones can overtake rational thinking and therefore men can make decisions that may not be in their own best interests. It becomes a situation where his erections over-ride his brain. This is hardly a shock to any woman who has had experience with men. These scans corroborate the research by David Buss showing that these behaviours are a universal, cross-cultural phenomenon.

> **'God gave man a penis and a brain but only enough blood to run one at a time.'**
>
> *Robin Williams*

How Women's Brains Rate Attractiveness In Men

Studies of women's brain scans revealed something very different to the men's scans. In women, several brain areas associated with memory recall became active when evaluating men for attractiveness. In evolutionary terms, this is an adaptive strategy to remember all the details of a man's behaviour.

For hundreds of thousands of years, women have had the job of raising babies to a stage of independence. Motherhood is a complex job and it is harder for human females than for any other mammal. Human mothers need support and protection when feeding and caring for their offspring. In prehistoric times, if a woman's partner died, she'd need to expend an enormous amount of energy to find a replacement. Unlike a man's immediate visual approach to evaluating the opposite sex, it's not possible for a woman just to look at a man and know whether he's honest and trustworthy, whether he can hit a moving zebra with a rock from 50 metres or if he'll share the meat with her. The same evaluative process is used by a woman today to be able to remember things such as what a man said yesterday, what he said three weeks or three months ago, how he reacts to children, whether he is kind and generous, how he treats his mother, his employment history and his assets, and she'll use all of this to evaluate his potential as a partner. When a woman studies images of one man, she recalls other men she knows who have similar features and then recalls their personality traits. Her brain then decodes the traits that correspond to the face of the man she's looking at. It's as though she is putting together a mental jigsaw of one man's character using a database of pieces of many other men. This doesn't mean she gets it right; it means that she constructs a mental composite based on the men she knows. While women's brains are recalling data about many men to assess a man's potential as a partner, men just take long, hard and many obvious looks at women. Now you know why women never forget and men are always being caught ogling women.

Around 79% of couples who intend to marry live together, but only 18% of these last more than 10 years.

Why Lust Doesn't Last

Donatella Marazziti, a psychiatrist at the University of Pisa, Italy, investigated the hormonal changes connected to obsessive-compulsive disorder (OCD) with a focus on serotonin, the chemical that has a soothing effect on the brain. Too little serotonin has been linked to aggression, obsession, depression and anxiety. Drugs in the Prozac family fight these conditions by boosting the chemical's presence in the brain. Marazziti was intrigued by how both the people with OCD and love-struck individuals can spend hours fixating on a certain object or that certain someone, and how both groups often know their obsession is irrational but they seem to have no control over it. She measured the serotonin levels of 20 OCD sufferers against 20 'madly-in-love' people. She then compared the results against another 20 people not affected by OCD and who were not in love. While the 'normal' subjects had the normal level of serotonin, both the OCD and in-love participants had about 40% less of the chemical. The way the scientists estimate this is by the amount of activity of a serotonin transporter protein in their blood platelets. This experiment can explain how early romantic love can often turn into obsession.

Re-testing the same subjects 12–24 months later, Marazziti found that the hormonal differences of lust had disappeared entirely, and their serotonin levels were back to normal, even if the couples were still together. Lovers will swear to each other that they will always 'feel' this way, but their hormones clearly tell a different story. Mother Nature is very clever: she adjusts our hormone levels for just long enough to drive us to achieve her evolutionary goal – to produce offspring.

Using the same method for volunteer selection, in 2005 Enzo Emanuele and his colleagues at the University of Pavia, Italy, investigated whether the chemical messengers, the neurotrophins, were involved in romantic love. They reported that the concentration of nerve-growth factor in the blood exceeds normal levels in infatuated volunteers, and that it increases with the intensity of romantic feelings. Like Marazziti, Emanuele and colleagues also found that after one to two years, all of the love chemicals had gone, even if the couples were still together. Neither the initial intensity of the love feelings nor the concentration of nerve-growth factor appeared to be an indicator of whether or not a relationship would last.

Interestingly, a study released in 2008 by a team from Stony Brook University in New York, headed by Dr Arthur Aron, scanned the brains of couples who had been together for 20 years and compared them with those of new romantic lovers. They found that about 10% of the mature couples demonstrated the same brain activation and chemical reactions when shown photographs of their loved ones as the 'new' lovers did. So there is hope for some of us.

> **For 90% of people, factors other than early hormone rushes are needed to sustain a relationship in the long term.**

Meanwhile, at Whitchurch Hospital in Cardiff, Wales, biochemist Abdulla Badawy has shown that alcohol also depletes serotonin in the brain. Low levels of serotonin dissolve inhibitions and create an illusion that the ordinary-looking person at the other end of the bar is unbelievably attractive.

All this research shouts a clear message to those looking for long-term love: wait for up to two years before making a long-term emotional or financial commitment to someone – and choose your bars carefully.

But, if all the chemical messengers of intense romantic feelings disappear within two years, what is the chemical glue that keeps some couples together for the long term? All is not lost – we'll discuss this in later chapters.

What Happens When You Get Dumped

One reason new love is so heart-stopping is the possibility and fear that the feeling may not be entirely reciprocal, and that the dream could suddenly end.

In another experiment, Drs Fisher, Brown and Aron carried out brain scans on 40 young men and women who were recently dumped by their lovers. As in the 'newly-in-love' study in 2007 by Brown and Fisher, the researchers compared two sets of images: one taken when the participants were looking at a photo of a friend, the other when looking at a picture of their ex. The results showed that when you look at a photo of someone who has just abandoned you, the brain areas associated with physical pain, obsessive-compulsive behaviour, risk-taking and controlling anger all switch on. They also found that when you get dumped, these brain areas usually light up even more and you become even more attracted to your rejecting partner. As a coping mechanism – similar to the 'fight-or-flight' response – your brain gears up for at least one more attempt to recapture your lover's attention to avoid the pain of being hurt. When, however, you finally accept that you have been abandoned and you come out of denial, the brain areas connected with despair light up.

> **When you get dumped, your brain wants you to chase your ex even harder.**

When the participants in the studies viewed their former lovers' picture, it also triggered the dopamine system in the brain – the same system associated with pleasure and addiction. This did not happen when they viewed images of their friends. The brain images of those who were dumped also explain why the breakdown of a relationship can trigger serious health problems. When someone is past denial and the happiness hormones such as dopamine disappear, they are replaced with the chemicals that can lead to depression and can reduce the body's immune system, triggering illness. The rule of thumb is that it takes about a month for every year of a past relationship for you to emotionally 'get it out of your system' and for your hormones to return to their normal stress-free, healthy levels. So if a relationship lasted for, say, two years, it would take two months to get it out of your system and for you to feel you are over it. This explains why elderly people who lose a partner after 50 years of marriage may never recover from what is commonly known as a 'broken heart'.

Summary

In basic terms, sex drive is the result of a cocktail of chemicals released into the blood by the brain, which stimulates the production of hormones, primarily testosterone and oestrogen. The circumstances you are under at the time can also trigger the brain to release these chemicals. For example, a particular song, a special smell or a person who has certain physical features can trigger the chemical release. As we age, these hormone levels, particularly testosterone, decrease. Testosterone injections have become common for older men and women with declining sex drives. We will discuss this more later, but it is important to understand that all romantic ideals, love feelings and the highs and lows you may experience in new love are chemically linked and are not the mysterious, mystical meeting of souls that many people like to believe.

Science is at last revealing things about romantic love, lust, sex and attachment that have been shrouded in mystery and fantasy for thousands of years. This science is like a GPS for love in the brain. Some people become alarmed about this and say that this type of research removes the wonder and excitement of new love and romance. In fact, it does the opposite. By understanding why you are motivated to make the choices you make, and by understanding that love has a scientific and biological basis and is not a mystical force, you can better control your choices and improve your odds in the mating game, in spite of the fact that your brain is hardwired the way it is. Instead of claiming, 'My hormones made me do it,' you can take control of the wheel and decide where you'd like to drive. In addition to your biology, other forces are also at play and you have significant control over these, which is what you will discover in the rest of this book.

> ## To not understand that love is a series of chemical reactions can leave you exposed to every love-rat who comes along.

When the first car GPS was introduced by BMW, some people protested that it took the fun out of driving and discovering new places. In fact, what the GPS really did was to stop people becoming frustrated and angry, spending time pointlessly in dead-end roads or driving down the wrong roads. It can be fun to be lost sometimes, but with new technology, you always have a back-up plan in your pocket or purse, and that's what's coming in the next chapters.

- In essence, our sexual urges and drives have remained unchanged in hundreds of thousands of years.
- Love, lust, romance and sexual desire are all chemical responses triggered in the brain.
- Science has proved that men and women view love relationships differently and that love is sited in completely different places in the brain in the sexes.
- When you understand that your urges and feelings are controlled by chemical responses in the brain, you can learn to work with, rather than against them.

Chapter 2
Straight Talk On Sex and Love

Some things haven't changed in a million years.

So why do we even have sex in the first place? You might think either there is a blindingly obvious answer or that it's a stupid question. Think about it – sex, romance and love affairs are all time-consuming and expensive pursuits. Dinners, holidays, endless phone calls and texts, lavish gifts, marriage, separation and divorce all take time and cost money. And for what? The reason is the continuation of your genetic line – and that's about it. It's all to perpetuate your DNA. For humans, sex, which is hardwired, also serves several side purposes – it's used to gain power, status and to play or to bond with others, as is the case with other primates such as Bonobo monkeys. But not all living things have sex to reproduce. Some plants, bacteria and simple invertebrates, such as worms, don't have sex – they simply clone themselves to reproduce. This is known as being asexual. The problem is that cloning produces offspring that are identical to the parent but are not stronger or better adapted than them; the offspring are therefore less likely to survive changing environments. An asexual female's offspring can only survive in the same habitat their mother was adapted to,[1] but environments are always changing. By mixing the genes of two individuals, you can produce offspring that are stronger and fitter than both parents.

> ## Sex is hereditary. If your parents didn't have it, you won't either.

This phenomenon was demonstrated in 2007 by Matthew Goddard at Auckland University in New Zealand. He compared two types of wheat – one that reproduced sexually and one that cloned itself. In stable environmental conditions, both wheat strains reproduced at about the same rate, but when the scientists increased the room temperature to create a harsher environment, the sexually produced strain did much better. Over 300 generations, its growth rate increased by 94%, versus 80% for the cloned wheat.

> ## Sex can be enjoyable and fun, but it is also time-consuming and exhausting. Ultimately, it produces a stronger, fitter species, and that's the main reason we have it.

How Times Have Changed

Up until the 1940s, age 42 was considered to be middle-aged. People aged 50 had only their retirement to look forward to,

---

1 Williams (1975).

and a 60-year-old was considered to be old. These stereotypes were challenged by Rod Stewart, Mick Jagger, Sean Connery, David Bowie, Cher, Hugh Hefner, Madonna, Joan Collins and Paul McCartney, to name just a few.

The 21st century will be a good time for people aged 40 plus as they were the group who were born or lived through the 1960s and the 1970s, which have had an enormous impact on modern living and culture. This is the generation who are exploring health and longevity, and learning how to turn back the clock on the ageing process. Until the latter part of the 20th century, a typical 40-plus woman was seen as settled, domesticated and married, and was more likely to use a bread slicer than a vibrator. Her life was considered boring and mundane, devoid of romance, sex and excitement, just like in the Victorian era. Now the role models for women over 40 reveal bodies and attitudes more like those of women in their 30s. This is the first generation of humans who refuse to acknowledge ageing.

Here are some statistics on the changes in some of today's societies. These were assembled in 2008 and taken from the various Bureaus of Statistics and Data and National Centres of Health in up to 30 Western and European countries, including the UK, Australia, New Zealand, the US, Canada, Germany, France, Holland and Spain:

1. The average age of today's groom is 34; the average age of a bride is 32. (Add three years to both ages for second marriages.)
2. The average age of first-time mothers in 2008 was 30. One in six couples now use IVF for conception because of low fertility rates.
3. The average age of divorce has risen from 37.6 years in 1988 to 44.2 years in 2007 for men, and from 34.8 years to 41.3 years for women.
4. Around 40% of children are now conceived outside marriage.

5. Only 36% of couples choose a church ceremony when they marry.
6. Around 80% of couples in which one partner snores sleep apart.

Results like these have never been seen in past generations of humans and they highlight a huge swing in our attitudes to relationships.

How Humans Are Now Studied

Humans are increasingly being studied within the evolutionary framework used by animal behavioural researchers. The labels for this work include evolutionary psychology, evolutionary biology, human behavioural ecology and human sociobiology. Collectively, we call these areas 'human evolutionary psychology' (HEP) because their shared objective is an evolutionary understanding of why we are the way we are, based on where we have come from. Many HEP researchers began their scientific careers in animal behaviour, and consequently HEP research is very similar to other animal behavioural research, being based on the principle that human behaviours evolved in the same way behaviours of all animals evolved. In HEP, the researched animal can of course talk, which has both advantages and pitfalls for researchers. Understanding HEP means we can better predict how humans will react or respond.

For example, the peacock evolved with brilliant plumage because peahens have always preferred males with bright, colourful, flashy tails. The peahens rejected peacocks with dull plumage because unfit male peacocks cannot grow spectacular tails. This has had the evolutionary effect of breeding out dull-looking males because females would not mate with them.

Just like peahens and peacocks, human sexual strategies for finding a mate operate on an unconscious level. As in other animal species, human mating is always strategic, never indiscriminate – despite what we may like to think. Simply put, women have always wanted men who could provide resources – food, shelter and protection – and men who failed to gather resources have less opportunities to pass on their genes to the next generation.

Why Being Loved and Being In Love Are So Important

Since the beginning of formalised medicine in the 18th century, doctors have been loath to accept any ideas about human longevity that couldn't be measured or quantified. Research now reveals that being loved and being in love allow you to live significantly longer and that no other single thing – be it genes, diet, lifestyle or drugs – can equal love's effects. Dr Dean Ornish, author of the groundbreaking *Stress, Diet and your Heart*, is a pioneer in the research of human longevity and was the first medical scientist to prove conclusively that ailments such as heart disease could be caused or reversed by lifestyle and by having positive, loving relationships in your life. He reported on the Harvard 'Mastery of Stress' study, conducted in the early 1950s at Harvard University, in which researchers gave questionnaires to 156 healthy males to evaluate how they felt about each of their parents, rating their relationship with a parent from 'close and warm' to 'strained and cold'. Thirty-five years later, it was found that 91% of participants who did not perceive themselves as having a warm relationship with their mother had been diagnosed with serious diseases in mid-life. Only 45% of participants who perceived themselves as having a warm relationship with their mother had any major illness. When it came to rating participants' closeness to their father, 82% with low warmth and closeness ratings had developed serious disease, compared with 50% of those who recorded high closeness scores. Of the participants who rated *both* parents low in warmth and closeness, an amazing 100% had been diagnosed with a major disease in mid-life.

People who feel loved live longer and enjoy better health.

Researchers from Case Western Reserve University School of Medicine in Cleveland, Ohio, gave questionnaires to 8,500 men who had no history of duodenal ulcers and then monitored them over a 5-year period. The outcome was that 254 men developed ulcers, but astonishingly, the men who had answered, 'My wife does not love me,' in the questionnaire developed 3 times as many ulcers as the men who said their wives loved them. In another 5-year experiment, the researchers tracked 10,000 married men with no history of chest pain (angina). The men who answered 'yes' to the question 'Does your wife love you?' suffered significantly less angina, regardless of their other possible risk factors. They also found that the higher a man's health risk category was, the more significant his wife's love was to his enduring good health. Ongoing research now shows that emotions play a powerful role as a buffer against things that cause you stress and that lead to illness and disease.

So does this mean that if you had a bad relationship with one or both parents you are doomed to die of cancer, for example? Fortunately, no. Research has also shown that an intimate, loving relationship as an adult brings emotional safety and can offset those early effects of parental deprivation. If, however, a person repeats the same relationship patterns they experienced as a child, they can become a strong candidate for major illness.

Studies everywhere now show that married people live longer, with lower mortality rates for almost every disease, than single, separated, widowed or divorced people. The chance of surviving more than five years after a diagnosis of cancer is greater for married people of all races, sex and culture than unmarried people.

Married men live longer than single men, but married men are more willing to die.

Early studies also show that married people experience better health than couples who choose to cohabit but not marry. This is because marriage carries with it more emotional security than cohabiting, especially for women, as it tells others that their partner is officially 'off the market'. Marriage equals less stress and more feelings of security, which promotes an overall healthier immune system. Linda Waite, president of the Population Research Association of America, conducted a study and found that for both men and women, marriage lengthens life span. Married men live, on average, ten years longer than unmarried men, and married women live about four years longer than unmarried women. In summary, married people live longer and have fewer illnesses than unmarried people.

> **By 2021, one in five UK couples will be unmarried, preferring to cohabit.**

The Seven Types of Love

For most people, love is a big mystery – especially for men. When a woman uses the term 'love', men have little idea what she actually means. She says to him, 'I love you,' and in the next sentence she says, 'I love sushi,' followed by, 'I love my dog,' and 'I love shopping.' So now he's left wondering where he rates against a California roll, clothes shopping and a Labrador retriever.

> **'Of course I love you,' he protested. 'I'm your husband – that's my job.'**

The problem is that most modern languages have only one word for a wide range of emotions called 'love'. Ancient languages had many categories of love and a separate word to define each meaning. The ancient Persians had 78, the Greeks had 4, and there were 5 in Latin, but there's only 1 in English.

Today, there are seven basic types of love:

1. **Romantic love** – physical attraction, sexual feelings, romance and hormone activity.
2. **Pragmatic love** – to love your country, your job, shopping or pizza.
3. **Altruistic love** – to love a cause, a god or a religion.
4. **Obsessive love** – jealousy, obsession or powerful unstable emotions.
5. **Brotherly love** – for your friends and neighbours.
6. **Common love** – for your fellow man and others.
7. **Familial love** – feelings of love for children, parents and siblings.

So the first time a woman says to a man, 'I love you,' what is he to think? Until just now, his relationship with her was great for him – lots of sex, laughter and good times. Now he's picturing commitment, marriage, in-laws, kids, boredom, loss of hobbies, mental torture, eternal monogamy, a pot belly and baldness. To a woman, love signals monogamy, nesting, family and kids – all the female priorities that can be scary to men.

Our Love Maps

A 'love map' is a blueprint that contains the things that we think are attractive. This inner scorecard is something that people use to rate the suitability of mates. How we decide who we are attracted to is determined by both our brain's hard-wiring and by a set of criteria formed in our childhood. These criteria are based on the things we saw and experienced, such as the way our parents said certain words or phrases, what they thought was exciting, appalling or distasteful, what our childhood friends thought was good versus bad, what our teachers thought about punishment and reward, and a variety of other seemingly minor things we were exposed to. Scientists who study how we make our partner choices believe that these love maps begin forming at around age 6 and are firmly in place by age 14.

But two things are now certain: women use a man's resources as their base measurement, and men use a woman's youth, health and beauty as theirs.

When you were four years old, you wanted to marry your mother, father, carer, brother or sister. Scientists have now found that we lose any 'romantic' interest in those close to us by about age seven, when people who are more distant, remote or mysterious become attractive to us. This aversion to familiar people operates on a chemical level in the brain, as demonstrated by the famous 'sweaty T-shirt' experiment. Women were asked to smell the T-shirts of a range of men and to rate their attraction to each T-shirt. The result was that the closer a man's immune system was to her own immune system – such as her brother, uncle or father – the less appeal the T-shirt had. The more different a wearer's immune system was to hers, the more stimulated she was by the T-shirt. This phenomenon is seen in other mammals and it evolved to stop us breeding with those who are genetically too close to us, which could lead to biological problems in our offspring. It's survival of the fittest in action.

Timing is also a strong factor in attraction. If you are experiencing emotional highs or lows such as depression, loneliness, divorce or are celebrating success, your brain searches for people who can satisfy the needs you have for love at that time. The changed circumstances alter your hormone levels and your love maps become activated. A change of environment will do it, too – studies show that when people are on holiday or at a work-related conference, when they are excited, relaxed and free of their usual domestic obligations, their dopamine levels are elevated, making them more susceptible to falling in love or starting an affair. In both instances, the underlying fact is that hormones are at play.

How Hollywood and the Media Colour Our View

An actor is a professional liar, and the actor who most convinces us of his character wins an Oscar. Hollywood is all about fake images, pretend romance and artificial glamour, but men and women are expected to emulate these images in real life. Actors create believable illusions and use special effects on the screen that can't be duplicated in reality. These artificial images have been pumped into our heads for two generations and have resulted in women taking drastic action to emulate the perfect goddess presented on screen, while men are expected to be more exciting, stimulating and romantic than they have been at any time in history. When was the last time you went to dinner at an expensive restaurant in a luxury limousine wearing Chanel perfume, Versace clothing, a Rolex watch, sporting the perfect hair and the body of a god, with a 30-piece orchestra playing in the background? Well, that's the image you're competing against and are expected to try to attain or expect.

These are the levels of unreality that are constantly being thrust at you by modern-day media, and this is the kind of pressure today's men and women are under and are being expected to live up to. Many women are deluded into believing they can have a rich Brad Pitt-type, while the reality is that they have a man at home who is a motor mechanic and earns an average income. The line between reality and fantasy has become blurred. At the beginning of a new relationship, many men, fuelled by women's unrealistic expectations, give women the illusion that they can reach some of these levels. Women want the guy from *Days of Our Lives* because that man knows exactly what women want and he always delivers. Before long, however, a woman realises that her man is really just a normal man and disillusion may set in. Unrealistic expectations are a significant contributor to relationship break-ups.

Women are exposed daily to hundreds of images of the 'new man' in phony romantic situations involving supposedly 'macho men' who think, talk and react like women. These men have chiselled bodies, expensive clothing, hairy chests and neatly trimmed beards, and are keen to listen to women talk about relationships and their lives. These images are reinforced by women's magazines, which make a woman feel that she must be the only one who isn't married to a hunky guy like the ones in *The Young and the Restless*. Consequently, studies reveal that women who spend their time reading romance novels based on fantasy never feel happy with their lives, although studies have also found that they usually have more orgasms than non-readers.

> **Why are married women usually heavier than single women? Because single women come home, see what's in the fridge and go to bed. Married women come home, see what's in the bed and go to the fridge.**

Why the 21st Century Is Harder for Men

Men born before the early 1960s were the last of a generation of men who were raised with the understanding that, to be attractive, they must always have a job, a hobby and an outside shed. They should hold open the door for a lady, never use bad language around any woman, drink lots of beer and revere John Wayne and Cary Grant. That's largely all that was ever required to be a 'real' man. John Wayne was the ultimate role model for men because he was rough and tough but he was respectful to women and fair.

> **A real man would never cry in public unless he was watching a movie in which a heroic dog died to save its master. Or if Heidi Klum unbuttoned her blouse. Or he accidently dropped a full case of beer.**

Since the 1970s, and with the emergence of more feminised Western societies, women's expectations of men and relationships have changed. Women now expect more from men than their foremothers ever dared imagine. Until the 1970s, a woman had to 'find a man' in order to be considered socially respectable, to bear 'legitimate' children or even to borrow money. Now that these conditions no longer exist, women are free to be more demanding in what they want from men. Many men have attempted to meet the new challenge, but because women's additional criteria usually mean she wants him to think like a woman – for example, realising when someone feels down, talking endlessly about feelings and discussing problems without reaching a solution (these things are not a natural part of male brain hardwiring) – men have been left confused and bewildered, and have retreated into what was previously called 'blokish' or 'macho' behaviour. These behaviours include an obsession with details about car engines, motors, computers or sports statistics and all combined with few, if any, personal communication skills. Today's feminised societies don't like this male behaviour and sometimes attempt to define it as an illness. Some males are labelled as mentally ill when in fact they are only displaying the acute forms of some masculine behaviours or have been poorly parented.

Today in education, teachers of young children are almost exclusively women. They encourage boys to 'talk out' their differences and 'play gently', as opposed to forming hierarchies, wrestling, play-fighting and electing leaders, which are hardwired male brain features. There are few, if any, male role models as teachers. It all adds to the confusion new generations of young men feel when thinking about what it means to be male.

Unfortunately, the bar for what women expect from men is raised almost annually by the media and Hollywood, to the point where many men have simply given up trying. Women are expected to live up to images of the perfect starlets on the cover of women's magazines, but it's even tougher for men, because at least women's magazines show you what you're supposed to look like – men's magazines don't. The new perfect male for the 21st century should be a warrior in the workplace, a metrosexual marvel when it comes to clothes, cooking and decoration, a stud in the bedroom, a six-pack god in the gym, a perfect dad, a friend who loves listening to women talk about their problems and a sensitive guy who cries when he watches *Beaches* and *Romeo and Juliet*. Unfortunately for most women, this type of man usually has a boyfriend.

As the list of requirements for the perfect 21st-century man grows, many men retreat into football games, car rallies and pubs, where men can still act like men in front of each other. Women simply go shopping and eat chocolate.

Summary

We now live in a time when relationships are more difficult to start and are harder to keep going than for past generations. Men's and women's expectations of each other are at unprecedented levels, and parents are at a loss as to how to advise us. Yet being in love and being loved are still as vital to humans for good health and survival as they ever were. Men are expected to be soft-hearted and feminine in some situations and bold and masculine in others, while women are expected to be self-supporting and know how to programme a GPS. These things were never part of our ancestors' job specifications. When you understand who we are and where we came from, you can develop strategies to successfully attract and manage the opposite sex. First, though, you need to know exactly what the opposite sex *really* wants from sex and love, and that's what we'll deal with in the next two chapters.

- Society may have changed beyond all recognition in the last century, but our needs and motivations have remained unchanged in hundreds of thousands of years.
- The media has given men and women unrealistic expectations of relationships. Nobody is perfect, and trying to look for someone who is, or trying to change your partner, is a recipe for disaster.
- Understanding our primitive motivations is the key to a happy relationship.

Chapter 3
What Women Really Want

Many mothers unwittingly train their sons to be lousy partners and husbands. A boy learns that his mother will love him regardless of what he does or doesn't do. She teaches him that he doesn't have to pick up his clothes or ask about her day. He doesn't have to take her to dinner or even talk politely to her. His mother shows him that love with a woman can be a one-way street and he's not expected to do anything for her to still be happy. This is why, when the rush of hormones associated with a new relationship subside – as they inevitably will – romance vanishes, passion disappears, and sex slows down. He didn't have to continually prove to his mother that he loved her – she knew it – so why should this new woman need constant proof? The first time it is evident that his new love has accepted the mothering role is when she starts washing his clothes, telling him what to eat and nagging him about what he's not doing in his life, and no man is turned on by the idea of sex with his mother. Understand that the only time a woman can successfully change a man is when he's a baby.

> **When you try to change a man, you take on the role of his mother, and she made him eat spinach and do his homework.**

The Changing Needs of Women

Today's women want far more from a relationship than their ancestors ever imagined. To demonstrate how much things have changed, here is an extract about sex from a school textbook called *Home Economics*, written in 1963 by a woman for young women:

> *When retiring to the bedroom, prepare yourself for bed as promptly as possible. Whilst feminine hygiene is of the utmost importance, your tired husband does not want to queue for the bathroom, as he would have to do for his train. But remember to look your best when going to bed. Try to achieve a look that is welcoming without being obvious. If you need to apply face-cream or hair-rollers, wait until he is asleep as this can be shocking to a man last thing at night. When it comes to the possibility of intimate relations with your husband, it is important to remember your marriage vows and in particular your commitment to obey him.*
>
> *If he feels that he needs to sleep immediately, then so be it. In all things be led by your husband's wishes; do not pressure him in any way to stimulate intimacy. Should your husband suggest congress, then agree humbly all the while being mindful that a man's satisfaction is more important than a woman's. When he reaches his moment of fulfilment, a small*

moan from yourself is encouraging to him and quite suffi-
cient to indicate any enjoyment that you may have had.
Should your husband suggest any of the more unusual prac-
tices, be obedient and uncomplaining but register any
reluctance by remaining silent.

It is likely that your husband may then fall promptly asleep
so adjust your clothing, freshen up and apply your night-time
face and hair-care products. You may then set the alarm so
that you can arise shortly before him in the morning. This
will enable you to have his morning cup of tea ready when he
awakes.

Some men reading this might wish for a return to this era; in
fact, some men think that the above text sounds fair and reasonable. The women of the 21st century, however, are looking
for more things in relationships than their foremothers
because circumstances were different in those times. While
today's women are still driven by their ancestral hardwired
preferences in men, they have also moved away from who their
ancestors were. While their brains remain rooted in the past,
modern society now allows and expects them to make choices
and decisions that past generations never had to make.

> **Mothers still tell their daughters to wear
> clean, stain-free underwear, without holes, in
> case they are involved in a car accident. Do
> mothers think that their daughters will be
> taken, unconscious, to hospital where staff will
> pull up their dresses and have a good laugh?**

Mamma Told Me, 'Shop Around'

In the 1950s, 60% of women lost their virginity to the man
they were engaged to or had married. Today, that figure is just
1%. One in five women born in the West or Europe since 1960
is childless – prior to 1960, women who could conceive did so,

as there was little contraception available – and over 2 million women now get divorced every year in China. A woman in her 20s today is just as likely to have a condom in her purse as a lipstick. Women who are now looking for sex are usually looking for a boost to their self-esteem.

> **In the US, 42% of high-salaried women are childless, and 14% say they don't want to have children.**

By age 30, the majority of young women have had 3 or more sexual partners. These women used their 20s to discover who they are, not to settle down and raise a family. Most women's magazines target women in their 20s with questions about their sexuality and techniques. There is rarely a women's magazine around that doesn't feature the words 'sex' or 'orgasm' on its cover, and women's toilets now have condom machines. Yet television soaps still have a courting couple married within six episodes, suggesting that the validation of love and romance is marriage. The dilemma confronting women today is that most men have hardly changed at all and don't match up to the men portrayed on television and in the movies. Many men still hold attitudes and have values that are similar to those of their fathers and forefathers, and are unwilling to come out of their masculine comfort zone of work and sport.

Current media hype tells young women that it's OK to participate in what was previously known as promiscuity yet, at the same time, today's women are also interested in or obsessed with permanent relationships and can't seem to get enough of celebrity couples like Posh Spice and David Beckham, and Brad Pitt and Angelina Jolie.

Girls Just Wanna Have Fun

The women who are leading today's sexual revolution, however, are not women in their 20s; they are the women in their 40s. They have a career that was established in their 30s and usually have children who are older and more independent. Many women have decided that they no longer need marriage and that being stuck in a boring and loveless relationship is not for them.

> **For many women, marriage is not for life any more.**
> **Life is too long. Marriage is for love.**

Traditional marriage offered women social status and a level of security because, until the 1970s, most families were headed by male breadwinners so women received a financial benefit. Traditional marriage no longer provides women with these things because they can now gather their own resources and achieve their own status, and a marriage can end overnight.

A third of women in the US earn more money than their husbands.

In addition to the new social circumstances today's women find themselves in, understanding how ancestral women evolved gives insight into how today's women think, react and value their relationships. Women always put love before anything else in their life, and they measure their success and self-worth by the strength of their relationships. Men, on the other hand, measure their own success and self-worth by their achievements and accomplishments. Ancestral women evolved as the carers and lovers of men because they needed the security men offered for food, protection and survival, and this was the trade-off. A woman who could not get a man to love her might be rejected from the cave and be at the mercy of enemies and wild animals. Women loved and nurtured their children so they could successfully raise this next generation of gene-carriers. Some males didn't return from the hunt or from wars, so women needed to give and receive love from the other females; they needed a support group for their survival.

This was their way of life for hundreds of thousands of years, and this situation has only changed overnight, in evolutionary terms. For the first time the introduction of the contraceptive pill allowed women to have the choice to work or have children. The Women's Movement of the 1960s gave women the opportunity to think and act independently and make their own decisions. The Equal Opportunity charge in the 1980s and 1990s brought women to new positions of power and influence. Nevertheless, the mind of the 21st century's independent, self-reliant, self-supporting woman is still plagued by the primal feeling of wanting to have a man in order to feel secure and fulfilled. This primal urge thrusts insecurity, self-doubt and guilt on the new-age woman, and she has no idea what's causing it. And herein lies the problem – it's taken around a million years for the hardwiring in a woman's brain to evolve the responses she is feeling today, but the changes to her place in the world have occurred in little over 50 years. Her biology is now at odds with her environment.

> **A successful man is one who can earn more money than his woman can spend.**
> **A successful woman is the one who can find this man.**

The Truth About What Women Want

Researchers are finally uncovering the real things that women want in their men, and these things are not always what today's women claim they want. What 21st-century women really want in men are the same base things that their ancestral mothers wanted in theirs – good hunting skills and the resources needed to successfully provide food and protect them and their young. As a result, today's women want men who have money, education, a sense of humour, status and authority – all of which indicate good resources. This is why women are attracted to men who are ambitious, intelligent, hardworking, motivated and respected by others.

Women today want exactly the same thing they have always wanted: resources.

Ancestral women wanted men who were taller, older, had V-shaped torsos and were physically coordinated – all signs that showed their ability to hunt and protect. Even in our politically correct, supposedly equal 21st century, women still prefer a man to have a nicely developed chest and shoulders – but not too big, because he could be egotistical or selfish – and a six-pack of abs would be a wonderful bonus. These are things that would be useful to hunt and catch a wild buffalo, or are used to carry heavy things or kill spiders, and are mostly irrelevant to the daily lives of 21st-century men.

Women's attraction to these physical attributes shows how their brain hardwiring is still seeking the exact same things their ancestors demanded.

So, in a word, women want men with *resources*. Most importantly, a woman is attracted to men who will share those resources with her and her children.

It's not just Monkey business

It was discovered in 2009 that other female primates also favour males who share their resources. Cristina Gomes and her colleague *Christophe Boesch* from the Max Planck Institute for Evolutionary Anthropology in Germany studied chimps in the Tai Forest Reserve in the Ivory Coast and found that chimpanzees enter into 'deals' whereby they exchange meat for sex. They observed the male chimps as they hunted and monitored the number of times they copulated. The males that shared their meat with females that were not 'on heat' doubled the number of times they mated with those females. This increased the probability of fertilising the females, and the females thereby increased their overall food intake.

Dr Gomes said this study finally revealed the link between good hunting skills and reproductive success among primates.

But it takes time for a woman to evaluate whether or not a man has these resources. It could take three dates, three weeks or three months. This is why women fall in love more slowly than men, and because of higher oxytocin levels, they also fall deeper. Forget the concept of the metrosexual man who gets his hair and nails done, cries during *Titanic* and likes to talk endlessly about his love life. He makes a great friend but not a solid life partner. The absolute bottom line is, women want men who can provide *resources*.

Having resources is the prime criterion for attractiveness in a man, the most powerful of all ancient female motivational

Today's woman still wants a man who can provide and protect – in simple terms, he has access to resources.

preferences. It has been shown to be as strong as women's inbuilt fear of snakes and heights.

Dr David Buss, professor of psychology at the University of Texas, heads the area of Individual Differences and Evolutionary Psychology. In his groundbreaking work on human mating, he conducted the biggest ever cross-cultural examination of people's preferences for a mate when he sampled the responses of 10,047 people in 37 cultures. He covered modern and primitive cultures and cultures that practised socialism, communism, capitalism, monogamy, polygamy and all religious beliefs. He found that across the board women valued a mate's resources twice as highly as men do. His research confirmed what all other tests since the 1930s have shown: women value a man's financial prospects as being twice as important as men value a woman's financial prospects.

Women have always needed to be able to identify cues to a man's resources or his potential to acquire them. Buss also tested 1,491 Americans using the same tests and got the same results as the tests carried out in the 1930s – women value a man's resources. We studied 1,295 ads in the personal columns of magazines and newspapers, and found that women list resources as a desired trait in a partner 11 times more often than men do. While men asked for health and youth in women, women sought resources and 'sincerity', which translates into commitment of his resources to her.

Women are attracted to high-status men because status is a clear sign of a man's ability to control resources. That's why it's common to see a champion boxer whose face looks like road kill surrounded by young, attractive women. Not necessarily smart women either, but young, attractive ones – that is, good potential gene-carriers. Think Hugh Hefner at the Playboy Mansion.

All surveys conducted on male and female mate-selection preferences show how women consistently give a high rating to a man's status, prestige, power, position and financial prospects, whereas men rate these attributes as low when selecting a female mate.[2] Women see these attributes as highly desirable in a long-term partner, but they are less important in a casual sex partner. These studies also found that women place high value on education as an indicator of resources, confirming the truth in the old cliché that women prefer to marry doctors and lawyers. In other words, he has no resources now, but he will have them soon. Buss found that women in every culture rate a potential mate's resources significantly higher than men do, ranging from 38% more important to German women, 63% more important to Taiwanese women and 87% for Indian women.

Women everywhere complain that there are few eligible bachelors available. Yet every café, restaurant, disco, club and office building employs unattached males to whom these women are blind. This is because the female criterion for 'eligible bachelor' is a man who has sufficient resources – or the potential to get them – to provide for her and her offspring, and few women believe they will find him serving coffee in a café, so they tend not to even notice him.

> **Women are generally blinded to men who work in low-revenue jobs.**

Wealthy Men Give Women More Orgasms

In 2008, evolutionary psychologist Dr Thomas Pollett from Newcastle University and co-researcher Professor Daniel Nettle conducted research that found that the pleasure women get from making love is directly linked to the size of their partner's bank balance and resources. They found that the wealthier a man is, the more frequently his partner has

2 Buss and Barnes (1986).

orgasms. Pollett and Nettle surveyed 1,534 Chinese women with male partners and analysed the in-depth interviews about their personal lives, including questions about their sex lives, income and other factors.

They found that 121 of these women (7.9%) always had orgasms during sex, 408 women (26.6%) had them often, 762 women (49.7%) sometimes had them, and 243 women (15.8%) orgasmed rarely or never. These figures are very close to those of women in European and Western countries. They also found that women's orgasm frequency increased with the income or wealth of their partner. While a number of other factors also affected women's orgasm rate, money was the most powerful one.

> ## The higher a man's income and resources goes, the higher women's orgasm frequency rises.

These findings are consistent with what we reported in *The Definitive Book of Body Language*. We discussed women's orgasm rate relative to a man's body symmetry and attractiveness, and the Pollett-Nettle study shows how a man's resources are an even more powerful force than his appearance.

Pollett, Nettle and David Buss all believe female orgasms evolved to allow women to bond emotionally with high-quality males by signalling to a man that she is highly sexually satisfied, and therefore unlikely to seek sex with other men, and so he should invest in her and her children. The bottom line is that men with more resources are more desirable mates and cause women to experience more orgasms.

The Top Five Things Women Want From Men

Women have always wanted men with resources or the potential to gather resources, so they have developed cues not only to evaluate if a man could get resources but whether he would share them. Essentially, women developed a mental list of behaviours that show a man could be willing to dedicate his resources to her. Only human males share resources with females. Other primate females must find their own food and protection.

Evolutionary biologists and evolutionary psychologists who study human mating strategies have found that women every-where generally agree on the important characteristics they want in their men. Here are the top five things women say they want from men:

1 Love
2 Faithfulness
3 Kindness
4 Commitment
5 Education and intelligence

1. Love

When you study the items on this list, they all add up to what women describe as 'love'. A woman wants to be reassured every day that she is loved and adored, and she needs his words and intimacy as proof. The list of favourite things a woman want to hear includes 'I love you', said in as many ways as pos-sible, such as 'You're beautiful', 'You cooked a wonderful meal', 'You did that well' or an unexpected phone call to say he's thinking of her. Showing appreciation of anything a woman does in the home is also decoded as an expression of love, and love implies a man will share his resources with her. In divorce cases, women regularly say that men take them for granted and never show appreciation of their efforts in the home. This is because a man feels that his efforts of being the main breadwinner (as most men still are), fixing broken things around the home, solving problems or changing light bulbs are sufficient proof of his appreciation and love.

Women believe that if a man really loves a woman, he should show it every day with his words *and* actions. Women want a daily demonstration of love. This is a difficult concept for a man to grasp because he shows the expression of his love by 'doing things' for her. He'll mow the lawn, paint the house, fix her car, take her to the movies, go to work and pay off the mortgage. The man's brain is organised to measure his self-worth and contribution by what he does or achieves, not by what he says or feels.

> **'When I got home last night,
> my wife demanded
> that I take her someplace expensive.
> So I took her to a petrol station,
> and then the fight started.'**

In *Why Men Don't Have a Clue & Women Always Need More Shoes* we showed how women's brains are better organised for language skills than men's and how words are a form of foreplay for women. Men need to understand that women need to hear actual words of appreciation and love to believe it is true, and to hear them daily. Remembering important dates like birthdays and anniversaries also rate highly on a woman's measurement of a man's love. Bringing gifts, however small, tells a woman a man loves her – and the simpler the better: a small flower from the garden and a handwritten love note or card are winners. The point is that a man's *actions* are the key, not the actual gift. Most men, however, feel that a gift must be large or expensive because that is how they measure the worth of gifts. For a woman, the gift of a handpicked flower from the garden carries more clout than receiving an electric toaster. Twelve roses may be perceived as a decoration for the home, but there is no doubt in a woman's mind of what a single rose means.

2. Faithfulness

Fidelity offers the promise that a man will continue to share his resources with a woman, but a woman's definition of infidelity is very different to a man's. A man is concerned that she might have sex with another man, which could result in him investing his time into raising another man's child. A woman's chief concern is about the emotional connection between her man and his fling. This is why her first question is always 'Do you love this woman?' In other words, 'Will you commit your resources to her?' The actual sex he had with her is not her prime issue. If a man says, 'No, it was just sex,' he will rarely be believed, because women cannot understand how you can have sex with someone without first having an emotional connection. But for men, it's easy. Men can compartmentalise lust and love in the brain, so that sex is just sex, and love is love. The bottom line for women is that sex equals love, which equals redirection of his resources. If a man says he'll be faithful, a woman feels that he won't share his resources with someone else.

3. Kindness

According to Dr Buss's research, kindness ranks third most desirable by women in 32 cultures because it also symbolises commitment. Reproductive resource is the key item a woman can offer, so she is discriminating about whom she will give it to, and love, sincerity, generosity and kindness are her prerequisites. Ancestral women preferred generous men and avoided tight-fisted men because the generous ones would provide resources and protection for her and her offspring, giving a greater chance of their survival.

Women who have their own resources, status and power still go for men with their own resources. Buss found that almost all women, regardless of culture, showed a strong preference for financially successful men, and that financially successful women showed an even stronger preference for these men because they want a man who is stronger than them. This is why you'll rarely see a rich, powerful, successful woman with a man who is a total loser. We conducted a survey of 624 European female executives and 86% said they would not be interested in men who were less successful than themselves, 9% said they would consider the idea, and 5% felt it wouldn't matter.

So how do the ageing female movie stars who couple with much younger males fit these findings? These are usually older, successful women who have a string of younger, less successful men. First, from an evolutionary standpoint, these unions have no value, because the women have no reproductive value, whereas a 60-year-old man and a 25-year-old woman do. For every 5 women aged 60, there are only 3 men of similar age available, so an older woman's choices are more limited, while older men have a preference for younger women – they'd rather a 35-year-old woman than a 60-year-old if possible. An older woman can feel young again with a younger suitor, but a younger man will enter this type of arrangement because of the benefits he can get – money, power, fame and notoriety. In other words, she has resources – money, status, connections and power – and he'd like to have some, please. This is not to say that a coupling between an older woman and younger man can't last – some do – but most don't.

Love Rule for Men No. 17
You must show heartfelt concern and public sadness over the death of your girlfriend's cat, even if it was you who secretly set it on fire and threw it into a ceiling fan.

Conversely, the famous union of Anna-Nicole Smith and her 87-year-old billionaire husband made sense – he was in it for the glamour and sex with a busty young blonde, and she was in it for the power, prestige and resources. He told her he loved her, and he showed kindness and pledged fidelity by marrying her. It's unlikely she would have married an 87-year-old man on a government pension who lived in a nursing home. If he had few resources, he would most likely only have married an 87-year-old female pensioner and that would be mainly for company. Interestingly, all studies demonstrate that men everywhere show little preference for a woman's economic status, regardless of how many resources he has personally. In other words, the CEO of a huge corporation is likely to be attracted to the same woman that the male junior clerk in the company is attracted to. Think of Bill Clinton and Monica Lewinsky.

4. Commitment

A man who promises commitment pledges he will continue to provide resources. Women everywhere accuse men of being commitment-phobes and love-escapees. When you consider what commitment means from an ancestral woman's viewpoint, it makes perfect sense. Sexual liaison for her would involve a commitment for 10–15 years to carry and raise a child to self-sufficiency. For a man, however, the same encounter cost only a small amount of time – maybe just a few minutes – and then he'd be off to his next venture. Because a man is wired to spread his genes as often and widely as possible, many men fear commitment to one woman and dread the idea of eternal monogamy, and most men understand that commitment means sharing their resources.

'I want him to show commitment' is the cry of women everywhere. It takes nine months for a woman to bear a child and at least another five years to raise the child to a minimum level of self-sufficiency for basic survival. Compare this to a baby chimpanzee, which can survive alone after only six weeks of life. As a result, women's brains became hardwired to search for males who will commit to stay around for a minimum period of six years to participate in the provision of food and protection for them and their offspring. On a subconscious level, men and women recognise this phenomenon and it is often called 'the seven-year itch'. It is detrimental to infant survival for a woman to couple with a male who makes her pregnant and leaves or offers no support, so women became hardwired to closely scrutinise what any male can offer to raising the next generation. To most women, marriage is still seen as the ultimate indication a man can give that he intends to stick around. Being the child-bearer, a woman makes a total commitment to the creation and nurturing of the next generation and she wants a male who will commit to the same. This is why trust is such a critical factor to women in a relationship.

From a biological standpoint, a woman doesn't want a male to be involved in the procreation and rearing of another woman's offspring, but to solely dedicate his efforts to her offspring. This is why being monogamous is a prerequisite in a relationship for nearly all women in contemporary societies. When a woman's trust is broken, it can be difficult to repair the relationship, and women who suffer several broken relationships can become cynical about whether any man can be trusted.

Many young women now use the word 'loyalty' in place of 'monogamy'.

It's much easier today to get information on a man's current or possible resources, but if he's not prepared to commit them to a woman and her children, then this is seen as a liability, because without this support, she'd have to fend for herself. The prime criterion a woman will use to measure a man's potential for commitment is...love. As we said earlier, research on love has shown that it exists in every culture in the world where love studies have been conducted. In the study by Buss, he collated a list of 115 'acts of love' as described by the women in his research project. The number-one item on this list was any act of love that demonstrated commitment. These included avoiding or giving up romantic relations with other women, talking about marriage and children, listening to her problems, being there for emotional support when necessary and the giving of gifts.

Sincerity is the most sought-after attribute by women in personal ads. Women ask for sincerity four times more often than men ask for it. Sincerity is another word for commitment, and commitment carries the promise of resources.

5. Education and intelligence

A man with higher education and intelligence is seen as being more capable of acquiring resources. Higher education means he's likely to hold more senior positions in the workplace and therefore have more power, status and resources. Higher intelligence promises the potential of the same things.

While women today are still hardwired to be attracted to men who are financially secure, they also strive for financial security for themselves. In past generations, this was not an issue, because marriage meant *for ever* and the man would always be there to provide for the woman and her children. And because past generations had large families, they also had the benefit of a large support network. Today, there is no guarantee that a man will be there for a woman tomorrow. For example, the number of families in Britain headed by a solo mother is 19.67%; that's 1 in 5 families.[3] This compares to 2.16% solo male heads of family, so personal financial security has become a real issue for women.

This is not to say that every woman wants to marry a millionaire, but she definitely doesn't want one who gambles, takes unnecessary risks with money or spends too much on himself. Past generations of women had little choice but to

3 Labour Force Survey, 2007.

tolerate financial recklessness and 'stand by their man', but 21st-century women see this behaviour as irresponsible and read it as a sign that he doesn't love or respect them.

Commitment – Why a Man Should Give a Woman an Impressive Ring

When a man wants to capture a woman's heart for the long term, he does it with a ring. And the bigger or more expensive the ring is, the more it signals to her – and to all other women – that the man intends to commit his resources to her. Put simply, the more outstanding the ring is, the bigger his commitment of resources to that woman is seen to be by *all* women. Even if a man is short on cash, he is better to take a loan and buy a significant ring than to give a woman a small or insignificant one. This is a point most men don't understand. A woman will look at her rings regularly and they remind her of a man's commitment to her. Female friends also look at each other's rings to gauge men's commitment. Even if the couple live in a modest home and drive an old car, the woman's ring was purchased specifically for her and is seen by women as a public declaration of the size of his love and commitment to her.

> Kevin understood how this love criteria operated in a woman's mind, so he bought his wife several impressive pieces of jewellery. Personally, Kevin wore only a plain gold wedding ring and occasionally a watch, and saw no point in wearing expensive jewellery for himself. He didn't feel the need to use jewellery to make a statement.
>
> Kevin's brother, Glen, applied this same male perspective to his wife, Leanne, and rarely gave her any jewellery, and if he did, they were usually small, crappy pieces he purchased in Thailand or at a garage sale. He was unaware that his attitude diminished her belief in his commitment to her because she knew he could afford to buy something better for her. Glen

also believed that the regular purchase of flowers for a woman was a waste of money because flowers die in a few days. To his logical male mind, a potted plant made much more sense because it was more permanent. So he bought her a potted plant – a rose. 'The flower of love,' he announced. In fact, he told Leanne she could take cuttings from it and sell them for money. Hey, she could even go into the flower business! To Leanne's female mind, however, when a bunch of flowers dies, it presents a new opportunity for Glen to buy another bunch and to again demonstrate his commitment to her.

Yesterday, Glen's proctologist removed the rose from Glen's rear-end and he should be back on his feet in a few days.

**To the logical male mind, a potted plant is a better gift than
a bunch of roses, and so this man sleeps alone.**

Because an act of love signals commitment of resources, it is placed high on women's lists everywhere. Almost all studies into the importance of love as a prerequisite to a long-term relationship show that worldwide 80–90% of women say they would need love for marriage or a permanent relationship. One study by Sue Sprecher, co-author of *The Handbook of Sexuality in Close Relationships*, and her colleagues showed that 89% of American women said they would not marry someone they didn't love – 11% would – whereas 41% of Russian women said they *would* marry someone they didn't love. The Russian result is largely because there is a shortage of available men in Russia, and because of the wider choice of women, these men are therefore less likely to want to make a commitment. In Kiev, in the Ukraine, we found that the average life expectancy for men in 2009 is 56 years, and for every

20-year-old male, there are 4 available females. Tickets to Kiev can be purchased from your local travel agent, gentlemen.

So our advice for men: you can skimp on many things in life but *never* skimp on any important item of jewellery you give to a woman. If you gave a woman a small ring at the start of your relationship because money was tight, upgrade it as soon as possible for a more impressive one. Whether you like it or not, it can affect your love life and other women will use it to judge your commitment. We found that the only women who will argue with what is written here are women whose men have given them cheap or microscopic jewellery and have refused to upgrade it.

The Last Ten Things a Woman Would Ever Say

1. Could our relationship be more physical? I'm tired of just being friends.
2. Go ahead and leave the seat up. I love the feel of cold, wet porcelain.
3. I think hairy bums are really sexy.
4. Wow, get a whiff of that one! Pull my finger again!
5. Please don't throw that old T-shirt away. The holes in the armpits are just too cute.
6. This diamond is much too big! And by the way, I've got enough shoes!
7. Take that block of chocolate away!
8. I don't care if it's on sale: £300 is too much to pay for a designer dress!
9. Does this make my bum look too small?
10. I'm going out for a while. Why don't you phone your ex?

Seven Simple Things Women Find Attractive In Men

The following seven points are also on women's list of criteria for a man's attractiveness and are cues to a man's ability to gather resources. They are not in any particular order here, but one thing is for sure: women are attracted to men who can and will do these things.

1. Women are attracted to men who make them laugh

A man having a sense of humour sits at or near the top of almost every survey on what is attractive to women and is regularly mentioned in the personal ads. When a woman laughs, her brain instructs her body to release endorphins – a chemical with a structure similar to morphine – which give her that warm, tingling feeling. Endorphins are one of the body's natural painkillers; they build the immune system and protect against disease. Laughter causes a reduction in stress hormones, such as cortisol, and it also lowers blood pressure, which in turn reduces the risk of heart disease. Increased cortisol levels suppress the immune system, so decreasing this hormone is beneficial to overall health.

Women subconsciously understand that a man who can see the lighter side of life will be good for her health, overall well-being and her long-term survival, so she will avoid men who are constantly negative and miserable or men who look like they've been weaned on a pickle. Men understand the power of humour, too – they compete with each other to tell the best joke. They know that the guy who gets the biggest laughs gains the most status at that time and that humour appeals to women.

2. Women are attracted to men who will communicate

High on every woman's list is a man who is willing to listen to her talk about her problems and feelings without interrupting her or giving her solutions. If you are a man, reveal personal details about yourself as she reveals things about herself. This type of 'mirroring' creates rapport and leads to intimacy more quickly. It doesn't mean a man has to behave like a woman, just to listen with compassion and without offering solutions.

> ## There are two theories to arguing with women. Neither one works.

3. Women are attracted to men who cook

For around a million years men have been hunting for food and giving it to women. Even in the 21st century, any man who can cook a meal for a woman will stir primeval feelings in her. This is why taking a woman to dinner is such a seductive event for her, even if she is not hungry. It's the act of a man who is willing to provide food resources for her that is the motivational trigger. If you are a man, enrol in cooking classes today.

4. Women are attracted to men who dance

The sole purpose of dancing is to draw attention to oneself, with sex as its base motivation. When couples dance, they often hold each other and mirror each other's body movements, just as other animal species do before they mate. Only one in eight men is equipped with a 'rhythm switch' in the brain, which allows you to sense pulses and click your fingers in time to music, whereas most women have this naturally. The purpose of most female dancing is to attract the attention of potential mates, nothing more, and any man who is willing to participate will be a big hit and never short of a date. If you are a man, go to dancing lessons immediately after your cooking class has ended.

> ## 'Dancing is the vertical expression of a horizontal desire.'
> *George Bernard Shaw*

5. Women are attracted to men who make them feel secure

Women feel insecure about three things: their appearance, finances and whether or not they are loved. A woman wants to be told she looks good, smells good, tastes good and feels good. To not notice that she has a new hairstyle or is wearing new shoes says to her that she's not worth noticing. Telling her how wonderful she looks and complimenting her choices of styles or designs makes a woman feel sexy and she might consider having sex. A man coming home late or not explaining his whereabouts creates suspicion and breeds insecurity in most women, so a man calling to say where he is or when he'll be back or that he misses her allays a woman's fears.

> **'Does this dress make my bum look big?'**
> **she asked.**
> **'No,' he said. 'It's all the chocolate**
> **cake you eat that makes your bum look big.'**

6. Women are attracted to men who like children

The reason a woman wants to be in a relationship is to be part of a unit in which she can feel secure, reassured and comfortable. The ability to create life is the trump card women have, so any man who signals that he likes children by playing games with children, pulling faces, being humorous or telling bedtime stories will score well in the attractiveness ratings.

7. Women are attracted to healthy-looking men

Women everywhere rate a man's good health as very high to critical on their list of desirable male qualities. This is for two reasons: first, if he is in poor health, he may die early or become incapable and this cuts off her resources; second, he may transmit the disease to her or her children through physical contact or through genes. A man in good health carries the promise of potentially healthy offspring and the long-term provision of resources. Women generally rate signs of bad health as anything from poor physical condition and open wounds to bad breath and inadequate grooming habits.

Good health can be observed by good physical condition, clear skin and high energy levels, which are indicated by fast walking and movement and a lively attitude (also characteristics of higher-status individuals). Laid-back, slow-moving males are perceived as likely to live longer but are also considered to lack motivation and ambition, and are therefore poor prospects for long-term resource value. So if you are a man, go straight to the gym to work out before you cook dinner for a woman and take her dancing.

Why No Woman Wants a Loser

Studies everywhere reveal that men who lack ambition are seen by women as very undesirable, and women will end a relationship with a man who becomes lazy, loses his job or lacks ambition. This is why a man who works hard and has career goals is more desirable to most women. Conversely, the same attributes in a woman are generally irrelevant to the majority of men because, as we will discuss in the next chapter, men see the opposite sex primarily as a healthy container for their genes.

To some women, this can make men sound cold and callous, but understanding its significance gives women an enormous edge when it comes to dealing with them in the game of love.

> **'Shall we try swapping positions tonight?'**
> **he smirked.**
> **'Great idea!' she replied. 'You stand by the**
> **ironing board, while I sit on the sofa and fart!'**

Women Will Always Want Resources

All wars are started by men, and warfare has only one goal – capturing the other guy's resources. Resources come in two clear forms: tangibles, like land, oil and cities; and reproductive resources, meaning women. Throughout history, warring men would raid the next guy's territory, steal his property, kill him and his sons, and rape or kidnap the women. Women were rarely killed, because they presented the perfect opportunity for the conquerors to pass on their genes.

Modern men's urge to gather and control resources evolved because of women's preference for men who controlled them. Men are regularly criticised by women for putting more time and interest into their work than they do their families. Women complain that men are more concerned with knocking other men out of the game and chasing bottom-line results than spending time at home with their families, but if women didn't have inbuilt preferences for men who can do these things, modern men would never have the desire to gather resources. Men do it because they know women want it.

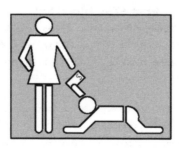

The new international symbol for marriage

Summary

Ancestral women would have closely examined the attributes of a potential long-term partner because a poor choice could lead to starvation, abuse or abandonment, and consequently, these are the same *base criteria* by which 21st-century women make their choices. Today's women still don't want to be abused, abandoned or treated badly. This does not necessarily mean that all women are motivated by the money a man has, but they are certainly *first motivated* to choose men who display qualities that will lead to resources in the long term, such as intelligence, status and ambition. It doesn't mean a woman will always end up with a man who possesses these qualities; it means she definitely prefers him. If a man has no resources or lacks ambition, then overall women aren't interested in him unless they believe he has the capacity to gather resources. So if he's a broke 22-year-old student who is studying to be a brain surgeon, lawyer or doctor, she'll see him as a good catch.

> **A new study has just been released by the American Psychiatric Association about women and how they feel about their arses. The results are very revealing:**
> **1. Only 5% of women surveyed felt their arse was too big.**
> **2. Around 12% of women surveyed felt their arse was too small.**
> **3. The remaining 83% said they didn't care, they loved him, he was a good man, and they would have married him anyway.**

- Women are searching for the same base things in men that their ancestral mothers wanted – good hunting skills and resources. Society may have evolved, but women's needs haven't.

- Laziness and lack of motivation are the biggest turn-offs for women because they mean a man doesn't have the ability to offer resources.

- Women want someone who can provide, who is good with children and able to make them feel secure.

Chapter 4
What Men Really Want

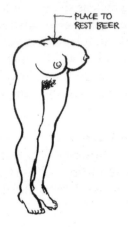

The perfect woman

For most men, relationships have little to do with happily-ever-after and are based primarily on what services a woman can provide. She wants resources; he wants services, so the basis of a relationship is simply an exchange of goods and services. When men are asked to describe the woman in their lives, they inevitably talk about the *services* she provides – she's a good cook, keeps a tidy house, is great with the kids, is an excellent entertainer, a good friend, sexy, has a nice arse and so on. In other words, services, which, put bluntly, he can pay for by the hour. When women are asked to describe their man, they say he's a good provider, is smart, makes me laugh, has a good job, owns a home and so on. In other words, he provides resources. Society presents this exchange of goods and services under the guise of 'compatibility' because it sounds polite and is a politically correct way to say it, but, at a base level, it still remains an exchange of goods and services. Men are simply interested in the services a woman can provide and her physical appearance.

If you are a woman reading this, you may begin to think that we are portraying men as shallow or self-indulgent. That's not our objective. We want to demonstrate that men's needs and priorities are fairly simple, and if you satisfy the right one at the right time, you'll have a happy man. If, however, you choose to judge his male 'values' against female 'values', you will experience constant conflict and continual unhappiness.

> **Men have only two emotions –**
> **hungry and horny.**
> **If you see him without an erection,**
> **make him a sandwich.**

Many people, especially feminists, become angry and upset at any discussion about a man's criteria for attractive mates, calling it superficial and skin-deep. They sometimes suggest, even insist, that any discussion about research into men's mating preferences should be censored or suppressed as it makes some women feel bad. The reality is that men's preferences evolved over hundreds of thousands of years, are hardwired into the brain and have hardly changed. The fact that men's preferences are based on physical beauty and youth has been necessary for the successful genetic advancement of the human race. Certainly, our society and how we now live have dramatically changed, but men's preferences for women have not, even though these preferences evolved to operate in an ancient world that no longer exists. To suppress their existence or deny that these preferences are real is like being angry at the weather because it's raining or being upset that carnivorous animals prefer meat to a vegetarian diet.

> ## To try to alter men's mating preferences is like telling them not to grow facial hair because it's no longer acceptable.

To accept that men's biology is a powerful, compelling force that controls their mating preferences gives you the opportunity to develop strategies for dealing with them. Fish evolved over the millennia to love the taste of worms and maggots. So if you're going fishing, it makes sense to use worms or maggots as bait because that's what fish like. There is no point trying to feed them what you like to eat – they eat worms and maggots – and there is no point expecting the fish to jump into your boat because you choose to think it. Catching fish involves understanding how a fish thinks and playing to it. In the same way, accepting how men's brains are wired to behave allows you to understand them better and to develop strategies for man-fishing and man-management.

How the Media Shapes Men's Views

The media, especially women's magazines, is constantly criticised for promoting a standard of female beauty to which all women should supposedly aspire. While this may be true for women's magazines, it's not so for men's magazines. Women's magazines portray celebrities, usually the thinner females with straighter body lines. The image of the stick-shaped woman comes from the fashion catwalks, where professional models act as coat-hangers for new clothing designs and the designers want the emphasis on the clothing. Studies show clearly, however, that the stick shape has little to no appeal to most men. This is because the straighter and thinner a woman's shape, the further she is from a 70% hips-to-waist ratio (something we'll discuss in more detail in Chapter 8) and therefore the less likely she is to bear children. Men's brains are wired to seek out the reliable biological clues to a woman's reproductive potential and are attracted to the hourglass figure. Men's magazines understand this – look at the magazines promoting cars and motorcycles and you will see curvy women draped over them displaying these biological signals. That's why you'll never see a woman who looks like a stick insect in a Harley-Davidson advertisement. Over 80% of viewers of the Miss Universe Contest are men, while less than 5% of fashion-show audiences are male.

> **My wife and I were in bed watching *Who Wants to Be a Millionaire?* I turned to her and said, 'Do you want to have sex?'**
> **She answered, 'No.'**
> **I said, 'Is that your final answer?'**
> **She glared at me and said, 'Yes.'**
> **So I said, 'Then I'd like to phone a friend...'**

Professor Douglas Kenrick and his associates at Arizona State University studied the media portrayal of biologically perfect women and found disturbing results. They found that men who were shown images of sexually attractive women then rated their own real-life partners as less attractive and were more dissatisfied with them than men who were shown images of average-looking women. Even worse, the men who had viewed the images of the highly attractive women described themselves as less committed, less serious, less satisfied and less close to their partners. Even the men whose partners were considered very attractive were still less satisfied with them after exposure to the sexually attractive women. These findings are concerning because the images of women shown in men's magazines and on the Internet are usually one or two pictures selected from possibly hundreds of images taken to try to capture the right image or pose. In other words, these images do not reflect the real world in which we live. In our ancestors' times, men would be choosing their mates from the actual selection of women available and would never have seen distorted or airbrushed images of perfect, fantasy women. It's a reasonable assumption that ancestral men could have described themselves as more satisfied with their women than 21st-century men because what the men saw was what they got.

Male brains still carry the circuits for this evaluative process in mate selection, but they are being fooled by modern technology, which over-stimulates men's response to ancient female fertility signals. As an analogy, fast food uses modern chemical technology to trick our brains into believing we are eating something of value that we need for survival. The results are diabetes, obesity and poor health.

The media images of perfect women are a contributory factor to why men have become less committed to relationships and are more likely to philander. These images also exploit women's natural competitive urges to attract men; consequently, women go to unprecedented lengths with cosmetic surgery, clothing and make-up to compete for men's attention.

Beauty fades – implants are for ever

What Men Really Want

There are four basic things that men have always wanted from women:

1. Sex
2. Basic services – food, washing, mothering, etc.
3. To be loved and be number one
4. Solitary time without interruption

It's that simple. Men filter everything they say and do through these four needs. If you can pick which of these needs a man wants at which time, he will become fairly easy to handle. The problem is that what's important on a man's list is likely to be seen by women as a low or irrelevant priority, and vice versa. For example, a man will see working late at night, working overtime or having two jobs as sacrificing for his family to provide food and shelter, but a woman may see these things as evidence that he's more interested in his work than in his family.

> **What Men Want Women to Know No. 153**
> Whenever possible, please say whatever
> you have to say during commercials.

In a relationship, most men will do the things necessary to get a woman to provide these four basic services. This includes romantic dinners, dancing, showing his 'feminine side' by talking with her and telling her she is the only one, the most wonderful woman he's ever met – you know all the lines. His base goal, however, is still to get a woman to provide one or more of his basic service needs, and to provide it now. If talking lovingly about 'together for ever' is what she needs to hear right now, that's what he'll tell her. A man will also lie to a woman about her appearance to raise his chances of getting laid because, among men, this is seen as a just and noble cause.

> **Never expect that a man will have you as
> number one in his life at all times. Sometimes it
> will be his friends or children, sometimes his
> favourite team, his car or his career, and
> sometimes you.**

What a Man Will Do for Sex

A man does things for a woman for the reward of sex and other benefits, and women know this. 'Take me shopping,' she says. 'Build me something, drive me someplace, take me to the cinema/dinner/my mother's place, put the kids to bed, paint the garage' and so on. How do we know men expect a payoff in sex for these things? Because men won't do them for other men. And if they ever do something for another man, a silent debt is established between them that is expected to be repaid at some time.

If a man is not having sex with a woman but he is investing time to do things for her, then the silent debt ledger comes in force, just as it would if she had been a man. He wants to be repaid for his efforts with either sex or future credits.

> *Scott was living with Kirsty and her two sons. He and Kirsty
> had been in a relationship for over a year but had broken up.
> He was unemployed and had nowhere else to live. He helped
> around the house – he mowed grass, did the washing-up, vac-
> uumed, took out the rubbish and spent time playing with her
> two boys. He bought presents for the boys, as well as taking
> everyone out for a meal each week. He paid her a minimal
> amount of rent, they slept in separate rooms, and he did not
> want an intimate relationship with her again, but Kirsty still
> loved him and wanted a long-term relationship with him.
> When he made it clear that that would never happen, she
> asked him to move out.*
>
> *He no longer visits and never sees the boys any more. He*

felt he had repaid any rent debt he owed to Kirsty and didn't need to go round there again.

The threat of withdrawal of a woman's services is why, when a neglectful, uncaring man unexpectedly gets dumped by a woman, he often pleads everlasting love and commitment to her, and even says he'll marry her or wants to have babies with her. He will tell her whatever is necessary to get back his food, washing and sex or to beat off a competitor. Fortunately for men, most women believe these lines. The lesson here for women is to enjoy the fun ride he's offering but don't always believe his stories.

History even shows that Sir Walter Raleigh put his perfect new coat over a mud puddle for a woman to walk across. Why? Because he'd been at sea for 15 months and was desperate to have sex. No man in his right mind would ever do this to his expensive jacket.

Men Don't Think About Relationships

As we revealed in *Why Men Don't Listen & Women Can't Read Maps*, most male brains are attracted to anything to do with 'hunting' skills, sex and spatial movements. The magazines men buy clearly reflect these needs – men read *New Fisherman*, *Which Camera?*, *Hot Wheels*, *Computer Buyer*,

In the beginning, God created the Earth and then he rested.
Then God created man and rested.
Then God created woman.
Since then, neither God nor man has rested.

Trader Boat and any magazine featuring scantily clad women. Men's magazines would *never* have articles like:

'How to Plan Your Wedding Day'
'How to Keep a Woman Faithful'
'How to Choose the Right Outfit'
'How to Find Your One and Only, For Ever'

Men's magazines feature articles like:

'How to Make Lots of Money'
'How to Build Perfect Abs'
'How to Be a Stud In Bed'
'How to Have Lots of Sex With Lots of Women'

Women read anything that involves people and relationships: *Woman's Weekly, Hello!, OK!, New Woman, Cosmo, Marie Claire, Mills and Boon, New Idea* and *Woman's Day.* And of the thousands of relationship books on the bookstore shelves there are hardly any dealing with what women think, because men generally aren't interested. Men just want to be fed, loved, played with or left alone. Few relationship books discuss this because most self-help books are written by women and over 90% of readers of relationship books are women. The main reason most men are poor at building relationships with women is because men just don't think about it much, and when they do imagine it, they often picture screaming kids, no money, baldness, nagging, a pot belly and eternal monogamy.

Most men, and especially younger men, secretly see a relationship as preventing them from taking the wild opportunities that may present themselves to them on any given day. Hey, if Tommy Lee had committed himself to the first groupie who dropped her knickers, he never would have had a romp in the hay with Pamela Anderson, Heather Locklear and many other gorgeous blondes, right? And even though these scenarios may, in reality, only apply to less than 1% of all men, they never want to burn their bridges, just in

The Perfect remote control for men

case. And that's how most men think. 'Till death do us part' is a scary concept for them.

> ## What Men Want Women to Know No. 43
> 'Yes' and 'No' are perfectly acceptable
> answers to almost every question.

Decoding Manspeak

Men have a repertoire of standard phrases they use to convince a woman to provide one of their four basic services, especially sex. Here are men's top ten lines and the translations:

1. 'You're pretty/beautiful/stunning.'
'Your face is clear and symmetrical, indicating that you could successfully carry my genes. Let's have sex.'

2.   **'You look gorgeous tonight.'**
      'I want to have sex with you as soon as possible.'

3.   **'Let's be friends.'**
      'I don't fancy you or I'm over you. Hopefully you won't call or text me forty times a day leaving messages asking where I am.'

4.   **'You look hot in that outfit!'**
      'That clothing highlights your hips-to-waist ratio and makes your boobs stand out. This all fires up my brain circuits and hormones and I want to have sex with you right now.'

5.   **'Like to come in for a coffee?'**
      'Let's have wild monkey sex while I'm half drunk and there's no bright lights to highlight any defects you may have.'

6.   **'Let me get you a drink.'**
      'Let me loosen up your inhibitions with alcohol so maybe you'll have sex with me.' The advanced version of this is 'Have another drink.'

7.   **'I can't stay late tonight: I've got an early start tomorrow.'**
      'Thanks for the sex. I'm out of here!'

8.   **'I want an open, honest relationship.'**
      'If I play up in the future, this line will let me say, "Well, I said I'd be honest with you."'

9.   **'I'll call you/meet you after the club closes.'**
      'If I don't get lucky tonight, I'll have sex with you instead.'

10.   **'It's not you...it's me.'**
      'It's you, so go away.'

As humorous as these lines are, the dilemma is that women fantasise to themselves that there is some truth behind them and most women encourage men to use these lines. Consequently, few women discover early whether or not a man is a serious contender for a long-term relationship. If women were to decode these lines for what they really are, they could better separate the studs from the duds.

Men Seek Reproductive Value

Ancestral men placed their priority on women who were capable of bearing the most children, and this could be determined by two observable factors: youth and health. The younger a woman is, the more children she is capable of bearing. A woman's reproductive value is high at age 20, medium at 30, low at 40 and nil by 50. This is why today's men have inherited from their ancestors a preference for younger women – because of their greater reproductive value. This is also why the younger a woman is, the higher risk she has of being raped. Statistics in the US show that 85% of rape victims are under 36 years of age, and this is directly related to a woman's reproductive value.

Universally, all men prefer their wives to be between two and four years younger than themselves, and the older a man becomes, the younger he prefers his women. In a study of the preferred ages men have for women, Professors Kenrick and Keefe found that men who are 20 prefer women who are age 18, a 35-year-old male prefers a 30-year-old woman, a 48-year-old male prefers a 37-year-old, and a man in his 50s wants a woman at least 20 years younger.

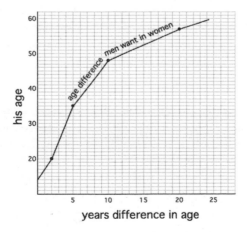

Instinctively, men seem to understand the relationship between resources and the ability to attract younger women. German ethnologist Karl Grammer studied a computer dating service involving 2,638 men and women and found that as men's incomes go up, they seek younger women. For example, he found that a man who earned €10,000 a month wanted women who were 5–15 years younger than him, whereas a man who earned €1,000 a month wanted a woman up to 5 years younger. Each €1,000 per month corresponded to a decrease of one year in the desirable woman's age.[4] In other words, men recognise that the higher their resources, the more mates they can attract and the higher their reproductive value will be. When a man is prepared to commit his resources to one particular woman, he increases his chances of securing a higher-quality mate because women who are desirable can hold out for the thing they want – long-term commitment from a man.

So does this mean that if you are a woman over 50 with no reproductive value, you are destined to be lonely? No, it means that, like younger women, an older woman needs to keep herself looking attractive if she wants to stay in the mating game. Women's magazines are full of articles about mature women and how they keep themselves looking young. Looking younger by taking care of yourself is what attracts men of all ages, not the fact that you can't have children any more. Think Joan Collins, Cher, Ivana Trump and Madonna.

What Men Want Women to Know No. 22
If something we said can be interpreted two
ways and one of these ways makes you
sad or angry, we meant the other one.

---

4 Grammer (1992). Figures have been updated to 2009 income levels.

None of these male preferences could be viewed by women as fair, sensible, politically correct or reasonable, but they are reality and it doesn't matter whether you like it or not. When you understand the origin of male preferences and that they are part of the male brain hardwiring, it makes male behaviours more understandable and therefore easier to deal with.

Getting to the Point

Men's long-term list

Here's what men look for in a long-term partner:

1. Personality
2. Attractiveness
3. Brains
4. Humour
5. Good body

When you compare this to the next list – women's list of preferences for a long-term partner – you'll see that they are very similar to men's, with personality being number one for both. The main difference is that women want a man who is also sensitive, whereas men prefer a woman to look good.

Women's long-term list

Here's what women want in a long-term partner:

1 Personality
2 Humour
3 Sensitivity
4 Brains
5 Good body

Ancestral women never had such an extensive list because all they needed was a man who had enough motivation to catch food and fight off aggressors. Ancestral man didn't need to be able to crack a joke to impress a woman, be able to play chess or understand her feelings. Ancestral women would have also had far less difficulty in finding a mate than women of the 21st century because cosmetics, designer bras and surgery were never an option. Our ancestors' playing field was much more level.

Now here's a twist that most women don't know: men have two mating lists; most women only have one. Whether a woman is looking at a man as a long-term or short-term mate, she uses the same criteria on her above list for evaluation. Men, however, have a long-term list *and* a list for short-term, casual relationships.

Men's short-term list

Here is their short-term list:

1. Attractive
2. Good body
3. Breasts
4. Butt
5. Personality

As you can see, this list is largely comprised of visual cues that cause hormone activity in the brain's hypothalamus and amygdale, so men's short-term list is about lust. David Buss listed 67 characteristics nominated by men and women as desirable in a casual mate. These included loyalty, sociability, honesty, wealth, kindness, intelligence, charm, education, generosity, responsibility and cooperativeness. He found that men rated these characteristics as dramatically less important in a casual mate than women did. Men were also significantly less concerned about negative characteristics in casual mates, such as promiscuity, alcoholism, education, bisexuality and mental abuse than women were. Conversely, men rated these things as significantly unattractive in a long-term partner. For long-term mates, men were concerned about the need for commitment and physical attractiveness, while hairiness and low sex drive were deemed undesirable. Men rated a woman's need for commitment from him as highly undesirable in a casual partner, but rated it as very important in a long-term or marriage partner. Even a casual mate who was married rated higher than a single one because the married woman was less likely to want a commitment from him.

A man's short-term list is the one in action in clubs, pubs, bars, the beach, gym and everywhere he goes. It's mainly a physical list because as brain scans show, men are largely visual and a woman's face and body are what he sees first. This short-term list is what many women respond to most of the time. Like it or not, however, it's what men look for in a one-night stand or short-term relationship, not in a long-term one. The woman who constantly dresses like a cheap tart or a hooker is responding to this list. Miniskirts, low-cut blouses, heavy make-up and raunchy behaviour are all responses to a man's short-term list. This is why women who present themselves this way spend a lot of time in short-term relationships with men. To attract men for a long-term relationship, a woman needs to study his long-term list and to dress and behave according to it, while at the same time knowing when to act on his short-term list to keep his immediate attention.

What the Personal Columns Reveal

The personal columns where people seek partners clearly highlight the difference in preferences between men and women. Men advertise three to four times more often than women do for a physically pleasing, attractive partner, while women seek resources as their main goal – that is, a man who at least has a job, a car and a place to live.

Psychologist Mark Mason at Nene College, Northampton, researched 2,200 personal ads to find out what is asked for the most and what ads are the most effective in getting responses. The formula he found was to talk 70% about yourself and 30% about what you want.

Here is an ad that has been shown to work effectively for men who advertise themselves as available:

Male, 28, high earner, sincere and genuine with sense of humour, seeks attractive, caring young woman for genuine partnership.

It works because it offers women readers what they want – resources – and asks for what he wants – youth and health, which equals reproductive value.

Contrast this ad with a woman's typical requirements, also from the personal columns and one that works very well:

Female, attractive, slim, loving and sensitive, seeks high-earning man with sense of humour, independent, sincere, for genuine relationship.

In this ad, she offers physical assets and mothering in return for resources.

Any discussion of what men and women really want inevitably draws howls of protest from some people and raises stories about someone they know who advertised differently from this but still managed to do well. Keep in mind we are talking in this book about the basic principles that are effective most of the time for most people, not about minorities or exceptions.

Why Attractiveness Has Become So Important

A cross-generational mating study over a 50-year period starting in 1940 measured men's and women's criteria for a mate. In each measured ten-year interval men saw attractiveness in a woman as very important, whereas women saw it as desirable in a mate but not very important. By 1990, both men and women were attaching around 50% more importance to physical attractiveness, and this rose to 65% more for men by 2008 than the same group who were surveyed in 1940. This is because greater globalisation and a wider availability of possible mates was available at the end of the 20th century, and the media worldwide became obsessed with showing perfect men and women. It also highlights that the importance we place on attractiveness is not permanently set in our genes but can change to match our circumstances. Unfortunately, however, we are more demanding of perfection than our forebears.

The study also shows that it is a species-wide phenomenon for men and not geographically limited. Latvian men want attractiveness, so do Greek men and Icelandic men, Chinese, Moroccan, Inuit and Zulu men. Men's preferences for physically attractive mates has been operating for hundreds of thousands of years, and these male preferences are completely responsible for the emergence of the multi-billion-dollar plastic surgery and cosmetics industries. These industries understand what signals trigger hormone activity in a male brain and so their products and services promise to deliver these trigger signals to women for attracting men.

> **A woman was standing nude, looking into the bedroom mirror. She was not happy with what she saw and said to her husband, 'I feel horrible. I look old, fat and ugly. I really need you to pay me a compliment right now.'**
> **Her husband replied, 'Your eyesight is absolutely perfect.' And then the fight started...**

Men also seek attractiveness in a woman because they want a visible display of their ability to control resources. A good-looking woman on a man's arm is seen as testament to his ability to get resources. Herein lies the motivation behind 'the trophy wife'. An attractive female partner can be classified along with expensive art, fast cars, gold watches and fancy titles, and thus makes a man more attractive to other potential females. Dr Buss's research found that, regardless of culture, having an unattractive partner decreases a man's social status, but the opposite has little to no impact on a woman's status, even if he looks like Mike Tyson on a bad day. If he has money, power and resources, he's still seen as a great catch even if he is shaped like an apple and looks as if a bus backed over his face.

What 'Attractive' Means

Attractive means that a woman has taken time and care to give her assets their best presentation and to minimise her short-comings. An attractive woman presents herself well at all times, and remember, men are first stimulated by what they see, not by what is real. A woman's physical attractiveness is directly related to her state of health, which is why men have always placed a premium on a woman's appearance. When an older woman dresses up and wears full make-up, she can be described as attractive but she is simply recreating the appear-ance and signals of a younger, child-bearing woman. Most women understand this, and the industries involved in cosmet-ics, weight loss, clothing and deportment carry the promise of living up to these male criteria.

Psychologist Paul Rozin conducted an experiment in which he asked men and women for their perceptions of the ideal female figure. He showed pictures of female bodies ranging from extremely thin to extremely heavy. Without exception, the women chose the thinner bodies as the most attractive and 'the ones I would personally like to look like'. To the men, however, the women with the average body shape were the most preferable in terms of attractiveness. This highlights how modern women wrongly believe that men desire women with thinner bodies. Overall, men prefer average- to above-average-size women with an hourglass shape. We'll look at why this is later on.

Interestingly, Professor Donald Symons from the Department of Anthropology at the University of California, Santa Barbara, was one of the first to report how, in a society where food is abundant, such as the US, men are attracted to thinner women, but in societies where food is scarce, men are attracted to plump women. He found that the mental state connected with food was most important, not the food itself.

Take a Leaf From the Amazons

To get men's attention, the women of some tribes in the Amazon and Africa go bare-breasted and wear a G-string type of belt that runs between their vulva lips and buttocks. Women of the civilised world would be shocked by this approach, but in reality it is little different in its effect to what 'civilised' women do to attract their men. They wear make-up to infer that their skin is flawless and healthy, mascara to make eye displays look bigger, lipstick to imitate blood flow in the lips, they dye their hair blonde to fake youth and higher oestrogen levels, undergo cosmetic surgery to make their faces appear younger and babylike, and wear push-up bras, miniskirts, nylon stockings, high heels and Botox their faces – all sales tools designed to appeal to men's hardwired preferences for youth and health. As we said, this also explains why men fall more quickly in love than women – visual signals are instant.

We are not saying to avoid doing these things; we are simply explaining *why* we do them.

What Men Look for In Beauty

Animals do not have a concept of beauty. No dog, cat or elephant has ever been amazed at the beauty of a sunset, a Monet or a waterfall. There are no ugly monkeys, cats or horses. In the animal world, what is attractive and beautiful in a female operates on a simple level – if she's on heat, she's a stunner.

How we humans measure the beauty in everything around us, however, has been handed down from our ancestors. We find a painting or picture attractive when it imitates the things from the world in which our ancestors evolved – water, animals, weather, conflict and refuge.

> **After returning from a check-up, 45-year-old Joanne said to her husband, 'My doctor says I have the breasts of a twenty-year-old.'**
> **Her husband replied, 'Did he mention your saggy forty-five-year-old arse?'**
> **'No,' she said. 'Your name wasn't even mentioned.'**

Men also evaluate a woman's physical beauty to give clues to her reproductive capacity. These clues include smooth skin, healthy, shiny hair, good muscle tone, clear eyes and high energy levels. These are all the things that women's cosmetics, shampoos, conditioners, creams and facial scrubs promise to deliver. These characteristics indicate youth and health, which equal her reproductive value. From an evolutionary standpoint, youthful, healthy women could produce more offspring, which gave a man a greater chance of his genetic line surviving. Consequently, women who display a high level of cleanliness are universally considered more attractive, whereas women who appear dirty are universally considered unattractive because filthiness is directly linked to disease and therefore a reduced chance of child survival.

Professor Randy Thornhill, an evolutionary biologist at the University of New Mexico, conducted an experiment in which he asked men and women to rate the attractiveness of pictures of women's faces. The older women's faces were rated less attractive by both sexes, with male critics giving significantly lower ratings than the female critics. This shows how women also have an instinctive understanding of how this principle works and explains why facelifts are so popular.

Our Universal Beauty Contest

The world has become a huge beauty contest between almost all women and across virtually every culture. More money is now being spent on women's appearance than at any time in human history. The focus of women's magazine covers is female beauty 94% of the time, as opposed to only 18% during the 1940s, when the main focus was on clothing, food and practical home ideas. The collective revenue in the US generated by the cosmetic surgery, facial cosmetics and dieting industries now exceeds $100 billion a year. The cosmetic industry did not invent images of women that men desire; it simply exploited them as much as possible. Feminists argue that women who submit to the beauty industry are unsuspecting fools who are merely pandering to the things men want or are being brainwashed by the media. The reality is, however, that the cosmetics industry and cosmetic surgery evolved purely as a result of women's competitive urge to attract men. Women instinctively know that doing these things will increase the odds of getting what they want. The worrying problem in all this is that the media promotes a level of beauty that is unattainable to most women. The effect of this lowers the self-image of millions of women and ignores the other main factors that men are looking for in a long-term partner, such as personality, humour and intelligence.

Our Reaction to Attractive Faces Is Inborn

In 2003, Judith Langlois and her colleagues at the University of Texas at Austin proved with their research how the human response to attractive faces is inborn and not learned through culture or upbringing, as was previously thought. She showed pictures of people with varying degrees of attractiveness to babies aged 8–12 weeks and a second group aged 6–8 months and found that both groups spent more time gazing at the attractive faces and less at the unattractive faces. In a second

experiment, she had one-year-olds play with dolls with a range
of attractive to ugly faces and found that the babies played
longer with the more attractive dolls and smiled more often at
them.

> **When a man looks at a naked model in**
> ***Playboy*, he's not wondering if she can cook, play**
> **the piano or has a nice personality.**

Interestingly, cross-cultural studies have also found that
there is a universal formula for beauty – that is, virtually everyone in the world agrees on what is a beautiful face and what is
not. In *Why Men Lie & Women Cry* we reported that the more
a woman's face is symmetrical – meaning one side matches the
other – the more attractive it is judged to be. As a person ages,
their face becomes less symmetrical, so younger faces are more
attractive.

What Turns Men On – the 70% Hips-to-Waist Ratio

We have mentioned this ratio several times because of its significance to men. Men are hardwired to seek out this ratio –
known as the 'hourglass' figure – and women who have it have
been shown to be the most fertile and have the highest chance
of conception. This ratio is used on almost every advertisement featuring women selling products to men. This ratio
attracts men's attention even when a woman is overweight. It's
the 70% ratio that counts, not the actual weight. This is
because a 70% hips-to-waist ratio signals higher fertility in a
woman and higher body-fat content – particularly stored on
the butt and thighs – is a signal of a woman's ability to breast-
feed an infant.

> **Many men think that the larger a woman's boobs are, the less intelligent she is. The reality is that the larger her boobs are, the less intelligent men become.**

Overall, men love women's body parts because they are opposite to their own. Where she has curves, he has angles. Where she is soft, he is hard. So when it comes to physical differences, opposites definitely attract.

What Turns Men Off About Women

The woman who constantly complains about what she perceives are her body's imperfections turns most men off. For example:

'My thighs are too fat.'
'My bum is too big.'
'I have too much cellulite.'
'I'm too fat/tall/short.'
'My hair is too thin/dull/messy.'
'My wrinkles stand out.'
'My boobs are too small/floppy/lopsided.'
'I hate my stretchmarks/pot belly.'

When a man is with a woman, he is usually motivated by her prominent body features and is blinded to her imperfections. If he's wining and dining her, being romantic and playing the courting game with her, he's usually so drugged up on dopamine and other hormones that *any* deficiency she may think she has ceases to exist as far as he's concerned.

Men are very basic creatures when it comes to women. It's not the size or shape of a woman's body that turns most men off; it's the size of her insecurity about her perception of her body that does it. An Australian study conducted in 2008 of females aged 13 to 28 shows that 86% were unhappy with the way they looked and would consider all options, including surgery, to change things. Today's men are tired of hearing about it and simply don't care. When he's turned on, her stretchmarks are soft and sexy, big thighs become beautiful, and messy hair is perfect, but a woman who complains about her flaws is unattractive to him. It's that simple.

Physical Choices for Gay Men and Women

Elizabeth Hill, associate professor of psychology at the University of Detroit, Mercy, and her associate William Jankowiak asked heterosexual and homosexual men and women to rate the physical attractiveness of a series of images of people. They found that both homosexual and heterosexual men gave almost identical results in their preferences for youth and physical appearance of potential mates. Heterosexual and homosexual women, however, placed little importance on youth in ranking their attractiveness. In their analysis of magazine advertisements for partners, Hill and Jankowiak found that heterosexual men and women and homosexual men were identical in that exactly one in three asked for a photograph of prospective partners, while only one in eight lesbians wanted one. When it came to offering physical assets in the ads, such as weight, height, eye colour, build and fitness, three out of four homosexual and heterosexual men mentioned them; one in five heterosexual women offered them. Only 1 in 14 homosexual women offered any.

In another study, Blumstein and Schwartz studied 12,000 couples, including 969 gay male couples and 788 gay female couples, and found that even in permanent relationships these criteria were still consistent. They found that 57% of gay men and 59% of heterosexual men felt it was important for their partner to look sexy, compared to 35% of lesbians and 31% of heterosexual women. The conclusion here is that both hetero- and homosexual males have the same mating preferences; all that differs is the sex of the partner.

How Governments Have Become the New Husband

Women's chastity and faithfulness are directly related to her dependence on a man's resources. In countries where governments provide solid welfare programmes for deserted women, such as the UK, Australia and Sweden, women are less dependent on men's resources because the government has, in effect, taken over that role – that is, they provide the resources. This is one of the main reasons that premarital and extramarital sex rates are soaring in high-welfare countries and also explains why extramarital sex is so low in countries that provide little or no welfare system, such as China and India. In those places, men have the resources and women don't want to lose them.

> *Andrew went to the Social Security office to apply for old-age benefits. The woman behind the counter asked him for his driver's licence to verify his age, but he had left his wallet at home. He said he would have to go home and come back later.*
>
> *The woman said, 'Unbutton your shirt.'*
>
> *So he opened his shirt, revealing his curly, silver chest hair.*
>
> *'That silver hair on your chest is proof enough for me,' she said, and processed his application.*
>
> *When he got home, he told wife about what happened.*
>
> *'You should have dropped your pants,' she said. 'You might have received disability, too.'*

Summary

Almost every study in the last 60 years into what men want reaches the same conclusion as painters, poets and writers have done over the past 6,000 years – a woman's appearance and body and what she can do with it are more attractive to men than her intelligence or assets. And this is despite the politically correct times we live in. The 21st-century man looks for the same immediate things in a woman as his forefathers wanted – her perceived ability to successfully carry his genes and to nurture him and his offspring. In a short-term mate, he looks for health, youth and availability. For a long-term partner, however, he prioritises personality, humour, intelligence and a nurturing attitude.

Unfortunately, in a typical week, an average man is exposed to over 500 images of 'perfect' women in magazines and newspapers, on billboards and television. Most of these images are the result of make-up and technology, like airbrushing, computer artwork and special lighting effects. Rarely do they show a real person.

What women really want:
to be loved, adored, respected,
trusted, needed, pampered, praised,
hugged, complimented, supported, consoled,
charmed, protected, embraced, worshipped.

What men really want:
tickets for the finals' match

Finally, when it comes to sex, what do men really want? The answer is, everything. Anytime, anyplace and under almost any conditions. A woman can find a partner for sex at anytime because she owns the egg. Men, however, evolved having to hunt for sex and to compete with other males for it and they were propelled by their goal of spreading their genes by reproducing with as many females as possible. This is why men became sexual opportunists. Today's woman still needs a reason for having sex; today's man still just needs a place. Now, let's look at what men and women want from casual sex and one-night stands.

- While they may not be aware of it, men look for women who can provide services – sex, nurturing, cooking, ability to produce children and so on.
- Men respond to visual cues – like it or not, looks are important to men.
- Just like their ancestors, today's men look for youth, fertility and health in a woman – all signs that she can carry his genes forward.
- The biggest turn-off for a man is a woman who is insecure about her body.

Chapter 5

Wanted: Meaningful Overnight Relationship – Casual Sex

Sunday morning, 6.00 a.m.

Saturday night, 11.30 p.m., at a cocktail bar.
(Turn image upside-down.)

Picture this scene. You are walking along the street when an attractive person approaches you and asks if you would have sex with them right now in their minibus, which is parked in a nearby private car park. If you're like 99.2% of women, your immediate answer would be 'No'. But if you're like three out of four men, your answer would be 'Yes'. This chapter is about why people have casual sex and one-night stands.

In 1982, just before the onset of the AIDS crisis, researchers Dr Clark and Dr Hatfield carried out an experiment on an American college campus. A reasonably attractive member of the opposite sex would approach a student and say that they had noticed them around and found them very attractive. They would then ask one of three questions:

Would you go out with me?
Would you like to come to my apartment?
Would you have sex with me?

While 76% of males agreed to have sex with the attractive female, almost none of the females agreed to have sex with the male, though about half agreed to go on a date with him. Dr Clark repeated the study in 1989, to see what impact the AIDS crisis had had on people's willingness to engage in casual sex. Men in the post-AIDS world were just as keen for casual sex with total strangers, while women remained just as reluctant, even though about half were still willing to go on a date with him.

We can assume that these women – undergraduates at Florida State during the peak of the sexual revolution – had unrestricted attitudes towards casual sex; however, a total stranger, regardless of his good looks, simply did not pass the initial threshold for a woman to consider as a mate. The study also made it clear that for most men, a total stranger is well above the threshold to meet his casual-mate selection criteria – with 76% of the men saying 'Yes' to an offer from an attractive woman they had never met before. This makes perfect sense as these men were operating from their short-term partner list and were immediately fired up on hormones.

This experiment has been repeated many times since 1989 with almost unchanged results. The more attractive the person who was making the offer, the more likely women were to agree to a date but they still resisted agreeing to have sex with him. For men, the more attractive the person was, the greater the likelihood he would agree to sex. While women were generally puzzled, surprised or even offended by this spontaneous proposal, most men were excited and flattered by it.

In another experiment, 99 undergraduates at an American university completed a confidential survey about their attitudes towards sexual intimacy. Among other findings, men were significantly more likely than women to report that they were willing to:

1. Have sex with someone they had known for three hours.
2. Have sex with two different people within a six-hour period.
3. Have sex with someone they did not love.
4. Have sex with someone with whom they did not have a good relationship.

This survey highlights how our immediate responses to sexual opportunities appear to have remained unchanged in thousands of years.

Kinsey found that 69% of American men had been to a prostitute and that 15% of these men were regulars, whereas the corresponding numbers for women were less than 1%.

What Is Casual Sex?

There are many different definitions of what casual sex is. Here are some terms you might have heard: booty call, hookup, anonymous sex, friend with benefits, fuck buddy, one-night stand and chance encounter. Call it what you like, it's all about one-off sexual encounters with strangers. It can also be an agreement between two people to have casual sex on a regular basis.

Initially, casual sex appears to involve people who focus specifically on the physical satisfaction of sex, rather than the emotional. Most people believe that casual sex lacks the emotional ties that come with relationships, and sex without any commitment or ties sounds very appealing to men, but as you will discover, this is not the case for women. The behaviour of some of today's women gives the illusion that their casual-sex motives are similar to men's, but they aren't. The only times women feel compelled to have casual sex for physical-gratification reasons are if she has a high testosterone level (and this applies to less than 20% of women) or if she is ovulating and her body is searching for the right male with the best genes. Even under these two circumstances, she will still have base-level criteria for having sex with a stranger. To desire only physical sex you need to be high on testosterone, and most women rarely are. Men always are. Women have deeper motives. We'll examine these motives in more detail a little later.

In 2008, Dr David Schmitt of Bradley University, Illinois, surveyed 14,000 people in 48 countries who filled in questionnaires about casual sex, how many people they expected to have sex with over the next 5 years and how comfortable they were with the idea of casual sex. The results were turned into an index of 'sociosexuality' – a measure of how sexually liberal people are in thought and behaviour. African tribes were not included, even though they are believed to be the world's most promiscuous people. In an index measuring one-night stands, numbers of partners and attitudes to sex, Finland was ranked as the most promiscuous country, closely followed by Sweden.

For countries with populations over 10 million, Britain was number one for casual sex and also number one for STDs (sexually transmitted diseases). This is thought to be due to the decline of religion, the impact of equal rights for women and the emergence of a culture that has become obsessed with sex, as Britain's moral pendulum swings in the opposite direction to its Victorian values.

The most promiscuous countries (2008 OECD)

1   UK
2   Germany
3   Netherlands
4   Czech Republic
5   Australia
6   US
7   France
8   Turkey

9   Mexico
10 Canada
11 Italy
12 Poland
13 Spain
14 Greece
15 Portugal

A Definition of 'Sexual Relationship'

When it comes to deciding what a 'sexual relationship' really means and whether or not a partner has betrayed you, men and women use different definitions. We analysed six main studies related to this question in an attempt to come up with a definition of 'sexual relationship'. This became a hot topic when US president Bill Clinton made his famous statement about Monica Lewinsky: 'I did not have sexual relations with that woman.' Legally speaking, he was right, because oral sex was not legally classified as sexual relations, but to the rest of us, he definitely did have a sexual relationship with her. Here's the collective definition we created that covers men's and women's attitudes to what a 'sexual relationship' really is:

Male definition: *any physical sexual activity,
including oral sex and full sex.*
Female definition: *any sexual, physical or emotional
activity with a person with whom you have a connection.*

From a man's standpoint, a 'sexual relationship' is anything involving physical activity, from intimate touching to full sex. For a woman, however, it's any activity, physical or not, that a partner participates in that establishes an emotional link with the other person. This definition ranges from foreplay, sexual touching and sensual dancing to secretly meeting for coffee or lunch, intimate emails or Internet chat, even if sex has never taken place. All studies show that men define sexual intimacy as physical sexual activity of any kind, while women see it in terms of its emotional, commitment and relationship connotations. This ties in with what we have stated previously in this book – men can see sex as sex, while women see sex as an expression of love.

Almost all researchers have documented that men are more enthusiastic than women in their willingness to have sex without any emotions or feelings. In 1990, anthropologists John Townsend and Gary Levy from Syracuse University studied 382 respondents and found that men decide on the basis of physical attractiveness alone whether they want to have sex with a particular person. They found that women consider a number of factors in making a decision to have sex, including affection, commitment and resources – 'Does he love me?', 'Is he interested in a continued relationship with me?', 'Is there another woman on the scene?' and 'Does he have money or potential?'

In another study, sociobiologists Ellis and Symons found that younger women are more likely to have sex with a man if he indicates he has potential and interest in any offspring she may have already or any she may give birth to. While older women are less interested in a man's child-support potential, they still use a man's resources as a major criterion in deciding whether or not they would have sex with him.

How long a woman has known a man also affects her decision to have sex with him. For example, the study revealed most women would consider sex with an attractive man they had known for at least five years, but most did not feel the same motivation if they had only known him for six months. For men, time made no difference – whether he'd known her for five years or five minutes, he was ready to go.

Why We Have Casual Sex

The downsides of casual sex for men are obvious – they could get a reputation as a womaniser, contract a nasty disease, be attacked by a jealous husband, lose significant assets in a cost-ly divorce or be faced to pay paternity on children they may not have fathered. Women risk getting a reputation as being easy, a moll or a 'slut', which is attractive to men for short-term sex but is detested in a long-term partner because of paternity issues. A woman who has casual sex also risks becoming a single mother, reducing her market value and imposing hardships, plus rejection by her male partner and losing his resources. The benefits to men are fairly straightfor-ward in evolutionary terms – reproduction. To achieve this goal, men want to have sex with lots of attractive women. This doesn't mean a man will do this; it simply means he is driven to *want* to do it. If he has 50 girlfriends, he could produce 50 or more children every year, which makes sense from a species-survival perspective. If a woman has 50 boyfriends, it makes no evolutionary sense – she can still only produce one off-spring every year. That means there must have been other reasons our female ancestors participated in casual sex. Some women's behaviour today creates the illusion that women who seek casual sex do it for the same reasons as men. These women get drunk, act aggressively and offensively, swear, pick up men and have one-night stands. Their actions look the same, but their motives are *very* different.

There are four main reasons why women, past and present, participate in casual-sex relationships:

1 Because of self-esteem issues.
2 To evaluate men for long-term potential.
3 To obtain a benefit.
4 To find better genes.

1. Self-esteem issues

Casual sex and affairs allow a woman to test her 'market value' and therefore decide how desirable she is as a mate on the current market. In ancestral terms, this information would have been important to know because if she rated herself too low, she'd end up with a mate who would provide fewer resources than she could have attained. If she over-rated herself – let's say she was a seven out of ten but saw herself as a nine out of ten – she may initially attract a man who is also a nine but when he eventually realised that she was really only a seven (men are not quick at working this out), he'd start looking for a woman who rated as a nine. Women whose partners cheat on them frequently often seek casual sex as a way of boosting their own self-esteem, re-establishing their mating rating. (We'll look at this in more detail in Chapter 7.) In other words, these women are getting a second opinion. Sometimes they do it just to get even.

2. Evaluating men for long-term potential

Casual-sex encounters also allow a woman to evaluate a man's potential as a long-term partner or husband. Women today who have casual sex are not subjected to the same social rejection as women in the past. A casual encounter gives a woman time to test a man for attractiveness, compatibility, resources, generosity and potential for commitment. In other words, she puts a thermometer in his mouth and checks his temperature. Unlike men, however, before starting a casual relationship, women are concerned about a man's existing relationships and his promiscuity, which shows that they are also testing his long-term husband potential. Men see a woman's promiscuity and her existing relationships as more of a positive attribute because they indicate easier, ready access to her, and if she's married, she won't demand a commitment from him. This is why, when women describe another woman as a slut, she goes up in the opinion of men seeking casual sex.

3. Obtaining a benefit

Looking at the hunter-gatherer societies that still exist in the Amazon, Borneo and Africa sheds some light on this aspect. Women there demand gifts in exchange for casual sex – food, jewellery, trinkets, seashells and tobacco – in other words, immediate resources. David Buss found that women want lots of gifts, money, an extravagant lifestyle and generosity from the beginning of a casual-sex relationship, but women rated

> **'What counts is not how many animals were killed to make a fur coat, but how many animals the woman had to sleep with to get the fur coat.'**
>
> *Angela LaGreca*

these attributes significantly lower if they wanted a husband. They want a potential husband to show kindness, caring, empathy and understanding first.

In ancestral societies and modern tribal cultures, the offer of casual sex from an unattached female could also offer her protection from attack by other males. In tribal societies where food is shared amongst everyone, women are twice as likely to seek casual relationships because the collective group supplies the main resources. In civilised societies such as Sweden, where the government provides the resources in the form of high social welfare, more couples are unmarried than married and both partners are more likely to participate in casual relationships than other Western or European countries where welfare benefits are significantly lower.

4. Finding better genes

A possible fourth reason for a woman to have casual sex is to obtain better genes for her children. It makes perfect breeding sense for a woman to want a man who is generous with his resources but who also has the best possible genes for her off-spring. The better the child's genes, the more likely that child will have a richer, healthier life, attract more and better mates and be happier. The wife wanted a man who could provide day-to-day care, protection and resources, but she also wanted another man's superior genes. Her desire for better genes occurs around the 13th to 15th day of her menstrual cycle when she is ovulating and her body is demanding the genes that will give her offspring the best chance of survival. It means she wants Hugh Grant at home for most of the month but her body wants Hugh Jackman's genes once a month.

How We Feel After Casual Sex

For most men, a casual-sex encounter or one-night stand can be quickly and easily put out of the mind. Men are driven to procreate, they are fired up with testosterone, and their brains can separate love from sex. For most men, casual sex is just sex, and this is a concept that female brains have difficulty understanding.

All surveys and studies about casual sex show that most men report high levels of satisfaction from it and tend to experience little guilt. Women's reports about 'the morning after', however, are very different. Most women report a lack of satisfaction, feelings of guilt and reduced self-esteem. In 2008, a study by Professor Anne Campbell from Durham University asked 1,743 men and women who had experienced a one-night stand to rate their positive and negative feelings the following morning. Unsurprisingly, 80% of men had overall positive feelings, compared with 54% of women. Men also reported greater sexual satisfaction, as well as an increased sense of well-being and self-confidence. Men were more likely than women to want their friends to hear about it.

Feelings of guilt are highest in women over 40 and this is mostly because they have been conditioned by parents with post-Victorian values or by religion that sex is dirty, disgusting or shameful. Studies show that younger women generally do not suffer guilt to the same extent as older women, but young women still report low levels of satisfaction and a degree of self-loathing after casual sex.

How Dads Influence Their Kids' Attitudes

In 1991, researchers Patricia Draper and Jay Belsky reported that the presence or absence of the father in the household in which a son is raised strongly determines that child's sexual strategies when he grows up. They determined that the sons of father-absent households will become cads, while those of father-present households will become dads. Father-absent families also showed a dramatic increase in a daughter's promiscuity and the early onset of menstruation. The conclusion is that these girls decided that men are not reliable for resources and as teenagers and adults were searching for resources by having an increased number of casual flings or affairs.

How Many Partners Do You Want?

The number of partners someone is likely to have is controlled mainly by the environment in which they live and the restrictions it imposes on them. Some societies encourage casual sex as a form of bonding or reward for visitors, as Fletcher Christian and his mutinous crew of *The Bounty* happily discovered when they landed in the Tahitian Islands in 1789. In other societies, such as some Middle-Eastern countries, it is customary for women to cover their bodies from head to toe so as not to invite unwanted approaches. In places like India, women who engage in casual sex can be seen as disgracing the family and can die at the hands of other family members in what are known as 'honour killings'. In most Western and European countries, however, women are free to choose their own attitudes to the number of partners they will have in a lifetime.

> **'I believe that sex is a beautiful thing between two people. Between five, it's fantastic.'**
> *Woody Allen*

Roy Baumeister, author of *Social Psychology and Human Sexuality*, conducted a survey of unmarried American men and women between the ages of 18 and 30 and asked how many partners they would ideally want to have in their lifetime. Men stated that they would like six partners in the next year, whereas women only wanted one. Within the next three years men wanted ten, while women wanted two. For a lifetime, these men said that 18 would be a good number, versus women's desire for 4.

Sexual Fantasies and Casual Sex

Most studies show that men fantasise at least twice as much as women during sex, but the content of those fantasies reveals a significant difference between men and women's hardwiring. Researchers Ellis and Symons found that 88% of men reported mentally changing partners or imagining multiple partners during a fantasy, versus the 57% of women who mentally switch partners. They also found that 81% of men focus on visual images as opposed to feelings, compared with only 43% of women. Men's fantasies during sex involve women's body parts, smooth exposed skin, sex with strangers and sex with multiple partners. There are two key factors in male fantasies – the first is that the women imagined are eager, willing and ready for sex, and second, the scenarios are devoid of emotion, commitment and extended foreplay. This is the perfect recipe for a male version of casual sex.

> **'Sex without love is a meaningless experience, but as meaningless experiences go, it's pretty damned good.'**
>
> *Woody Allen*

Women's fantasies during sex involve focusing on the emotions and personality of the imagined partner (57%), and the subject of their fantasy is usually someone they know, know of or are involved with. Rarely do they ever involve casual sex with strangers, even though a common fantasy for women is sex with a group of James Bond lookalikes. But this fantasy has to do with power issues – the woman is controlling the men with her femininity. As we have stated, for most men sex is sex and love is love, and sometimes they happen together.

Fantasies occurring in dreams are about the only place where men and women approach any degree of sexual equality. Dr Antonio Zadra at the Dream and Nightmare Laboratory in Montreal studied more than 3,500 dream reports from men and women, and found that the sex content of their dreams was 8% for both. Having sex was the most common type of sex dream, followed by sexual advances, kissing and fantasies, and both men and women reported experiencing an orgasm in 4% of their sexual dreams. Current or past partners were in 20% of women's sexual dreams, and public figures or movie stars – that is, men with resources –

were twice as likely to be the focus in women's dreams. Well-known women only featured in 14% of men's dreams, whereas multiple sexual partners were reported twice as frequently.

For most women, however, sex and love always go together, even in fantasies.

> **'Women go after doctors like men go after models. Women want someone with the knowledge of the body; men just want the body.'**
>
> *Seinfeld*

How Gay Men and Women Look At Things

Donald Symons conducted research on gay men and women, and revealed some interesting perspectives into heterosexual preferences. He found that single gay men's sexuality was unconstrained by the rules imposed on straight men by straight women regarding commitment, involvement and romance. In other words, because single gay men have none of the rules, they can go for it hard, fast and as often as they like with as many new partners as they choose. Heterosexual men would love to have this opportunity but straight women usually won't allow it. For gay men in a committed 'married' relationship, however, the same fidelity rules apply that apply to straight married couples.

Symons also found that gay women behave in a relationship like straight women and impose the same commitment and fidelity rules on their partners. In his landmark research into sexual behaviour, Alfred Kinsey found that 94% of gay men had had over 15 partners, and almost half gay men had over 500 sexual partners in a lifetime – mostly strangers met in bars, toilets, gay clubs and steam baths – whereas only 15% of homosexual women had that many. They prefer intimate, lasting, committed relationships, just as straight women do. We are not saying that gay men can't or don't have committed relationships – many do; it's just that they don't have the same constraints placed on them as straight men.

Summary

The main reason men have casual sex is for sexual variety, and they will do it when the risks are low. Men are opportunists and seldom plan casual sex. All studies show that, across most cultures, men are twice as likely as women to have casual sex or an affair. The main reason women have casual sex is due to lack of love, which causes self-esteem issues, to test-run a man for future potential or for getting something they want.

When human sexual motives are examined in the cold, hard light of day, it is often in contradiction to the warm, fuzzy images presented to us in romance books, women's magazines and on television. Women everywhere are confounded and confused by the ease that men will have sex with women they hardly know or don't even like. Men should also be aware that women trade sex for benefits and are always on the lookout for a better offer, especially if a man knowingly allows his Mating Rating to decline.

Casual sex operates in the primitive part of the brain and is hormone-driven. If it moves from lust to the romantic love stage, it can be classified as an affair, and that's what we'll discuss in the next chapter.

- Men and women have completely different views of casual sex.
- Men are driven to procreate, and so for them, sex can be just sex. This is why men have so many more one-night stands than women.
- Women, however, are in the main unable to separate love from sex.

Chapter 6
Your Place or Mine?
Affairs and Cheating

Colin and Jill married five years ago. Following their honeymoon, they described their sex life as 'absolutely incredible', and they were always 'going at it like rabbits'. When Jill was six months into her first pregnancy, things started to go wrong for them. She thought she looked fat, frumpy and undesirable, so began to avoid sex, telling Colin she didn't feel well, had a headache or, 'Maybe tomorrow.' She wanted to talk with him about her feelings and emotions, but Colin figured she needed time alone – his male brain was not wired to understand the importance of talking and listening to her. This made her feel that he didn't care about her and that he just treated her as a sex object. As a consequence, Colin felt rejected. His frustration at the lack of sex began to turn to resentment – he no longer felt masculine. He perceived her

emotional outbursts as attacks on him personally and she saw his anger towards her as proof of how fat and frumpy she must be.

After the baby was born, things went from bad to worse. Jill was constantly occupied with the new baby and Colin started to feel that she was punishing him and forcing him into second place, with the new baby becoming number one. After a while, he became so upset about it that he thought the dog now occupied second place, with him as a distant third. Colin began an affair with Alison at the office and Jill left him. Jill now lives alone with her new son. Colin struggles to financially maintain Jill and their child and his new life.

The thought of a partner having an affair is one of the biggest concerns for people in a long-term relationship, yet few really understand the reasons why affairs begin. Colin and Jill's break-up highlights a vicious circle experienced by many couples. Colin didn't understand that a woman needs to feel in the mood to have sex. She wants a man to talk with her about her feelings and emotions, to listen with compassion and touch her tenderly – all things that are not part of his basic hard-wiring. For Jill, the problems were amplified by hormonal changes, and her self-image was taking a beating because she thought she looked fat and frumpy. Jill didn't understand that men express themselves emotionally through sex and that the male brain can separate love from sex. For men, love can be love and sex can be just sex, and sometimes they happen together. As a result, she blamed Colin for being insensitive and uncaring. He blamed her for being sexually manipulative and frigid. Soon it became a habit: he expected his advances to be rejected by her, and she expected him to be aloof and uncaring. The reality was that he felt rejected and isolated, and she felt insecure and unattractive. She developed a fear of having sex and avoided Colin. He developed a fear of rejection, so stopped asking for sex. Neither understood the other's perspective and a perfectly viable relationship ended.

What Is an Affair?

In this chapter, we will use the word 'marriage' to describe any relationship in which two people agree to be faithful to each other. Technically speaking, they have moved from lust into the romantic love or long-term attachment stages, when brain chemistry changes.

Casual sex is about lust. As discussed in Chapter 1, two parts of the brain become very active during lust – the hypothalamus (primordial drives) and the amygdale (arousal). Dopamine is heavily secreted during lust and triggers the production of testosterone, creating sexual stimulation. When a casual fling (lust) moves to the next stage – romantic love – it signals the internal beginnings of an 'affair'. With women, the brain activates the caudate, causing her testosterone levels to rise, increasing her sexual desire.

Different areas of the brain become active in men, including the visual cortex, and a man's oxytocin level rises, making him softer and cuddlier. These temporary chemical reactions give the couple the illusion that they are perfectly matched. The main difference between men and women is that men usually stay in the lust stage longer than women, which means that while he's still in it for the sex, she's moved on to the next stage.

When men are asked to define an affair, they tend to describe it as ongoing sex with or without emotional connection, in the same way they view casual sex. Men see an affair as *physical* involvement, not necessarily having an emotional connection.

Women, however, see an affair as an emotional event, whether it involves physical sex or not, and it is often called an 'emotional affair'. It includes talking on the phone, sharing personal emails or intimate texting, regularly going to lunch or coffee and so on. An emotional affair is a relationship between two people other than a spouse or lover that impacts on the level of intimacy, emotional distance and overall balance of their marriage. The partner being unfaithful may spend an inappropriate or an excessive amount of time with someone of the opposite (or same) sex. That is time, emotional energy and care taken away from the faithful partner. He or she may confide more in their new 'friend' than in their permanent partner and may share more intimate emotional feelings and secrets with them. This type of relationship is not necessarily physically intimate in the beginning but almost inevitably leads to a physical relationship. To the majority of women, however, it's still an affair. Sex only emphasises the pain because it demonstrates the depth of the emotional affair.

> **Most men think that unless they are having sex with another woman, they are not doing anything wrong.**

Your Cheating Heart

A 2006 survey showed that infidelity was the most cited cause for divorce in a survey of 150 cultures. No one really knows how many people are cheaters because if people will lie to their partner, it's unlikely they'll be honest in surveys. For example, in 2007, researchers from the University of Colorado and Texas A&M University surveyed 4,884 married women using face-to-face interviews plus anonymous computer questionnaires. In the face-to-face interviews, only 1% of women said they had been unfaithful to their husbands in the past year; in the computer questionnaire, more than 6% of the same group said they had been unfaithful.

The most consistent data on infidelity comes from the General Social Survey conducted by the National Science Foundation at the University of Chicago, which has tracked the opinions and social behaviour of Americans since 1972. The survey data showed that in any given year about 10% of married people – 12% of men, and 7% of women – say they have had sex outside their marriage. In most Western and European countries, 50–60% of males are estimated to have been unfaithful at least once, and in places like France and Sweden, it's around 70–80% of men. About 40% of these affairs will be discovered, and the rest will probably get away with it. Around 40% of married women will also indulge in horizontal folk dancing, while only 15% will be discovered. The only place in the world where women overtake men in affairs is France, where 87% of women admit to two-timing a partner, either in a current or past relationship.

Infidelity is on the rise in all age groups – between 1998 and 2008 in the US, it rose by 20% for men over 60 and 15% for women. So why is the older generation doing the horizontal hula like never before? Two reasons: first, the Baby Boomers are in this group, who rejected Victorian attitudes to sex and refuse to accept getting old – they see age 60 as the new 45; second, older people now have some things past generations never had – Viagra, hormone-replacement therapy (HRT) and erectile-dysfunction solutions. The 40- to 60-year-old group is the last of the Baby Boomers, who – especially women – are throwing off the restrictive sexual constraints of their past.

Infidelity is also up in the under-40s group, and this is driven by the widespread availability of Internet porn, which is changing what this group sees as 'normal' sexual behaviour – past generations never heard the words 'fisting', 'scat', 'MILF' or 'cruising the Hershey Highway'. In 2002, psychologists Raymond Bergner and Ana Bridges were the first to show how Internet porn had a significantly negative effect on permanent relationships. They found that the emotional distance created by Internet porn and online sexual relationships can be just as damaging to a relationship as real-life sexual infidelity.

> **'I'm so depressed. My doctor refused to write me a prescription for Viagra. He said it would be like putting a new flagpole on a condemned building.'**
>
> *George Burns*

Dr David Schmitt of Bradley University, Illinois, collected data on the sexual habits of men and women from 48 countries across the world and found that men dunk the love muscle more in their late 20s than at any other age. This is the time when male testosterone has peaked and has begun its decline. Women are more likely to philander in their 30s because their biological clock starts ticking as their fertility reduces. Women reach their sexual peak in their mid- to late 30s, when testosterone levels rise, and this is Nature's way of pushing women to reproduce before time runs out.

Analysing the results of most infidelity surveys will bring you to the conclusion that around 50% of men and 30% of women have probably dropped their drawers at least once while a partner wasn't looking. That's a lot of infidelity. It's important to remember, however, that these statistics also mean that most people are still faithful most of the time.

> **A man had six children and was so proud of himself that he started calling his wife 'Mother of Six', in spite of her objections to this name. One night at a restaurant he shouted at the top of his voice, 'Shall we go home now, Mother of Six?' Irritated by his lack of discretion, she yelled back, 'Anytime you're ready, Father of Four.'**

Why Affairs Happen

A poll of the clients of divorce lawyers in the UK in 2008 showed the top ten reasons men gave for playing around were:

1　Lust
2　Loss of attraction to their wife/partner
3　Sex problems – they want more sex or more variety or have a sex addiction
4　Wife preoccupied by family life and the demands of children
5　Aggressive seduction by another woman
6　Lack of aggressive seduction by their partner
7　Thrill of the chase
8　Nagging
9　Failure to communicate with partner about problems
10　Male self-image – sex appeal, ageing, an easy ego-boost

By contrast, what most women are looking for is more akin to an out-of-body experience. They want to be someone other than wife, mother, daughter or employee. They want to be with someone who makes demands of them other than 'Take my suit to the cleaner's', 'Have you packed my lunch box?' and 'Have I got a clean shirt for the meeting?' Even women who are not at home but have successful careers of their own and are respected at work find they are underestimated and often unappreciated in their own home.

For some women, it's simply a way of making a man stand

up and take notice, drag him back to the romance of their earlier life, remind him they are more than just housewives or pay him back for an affair he had. Women are also looking to boost their egos – they want to feel needed, desirable, that a man thinks it's worth taking risks for them, that they merit the time spent on foreplay and so on. For women cheaters, sex is not their driving force; it's emotional nourishment.

> **'Men supplement their marriages with extra-marital sex; women augment their marriages with some extra emotional nourishment, which also includes sex.'**
>
> *Debbie Then*, Women Who Stay With Men Who Stray

The top ten answers women gave when asked why they had an affair were:

1 Loneliness (the most common problem for stay-at-home women)
2 Unable to communicate with their partner about problems
3 Not made to feel desirable enough
4 Lack of appreciation by husband
5 Husband too self-absorbed and full of hang-ups
6 Lack of romance and excitement in bed
7 Need to escape the routine in their life
8 Wanted to feel as powerful in their personal life as at work
9 Bored of routine
10 Opportunity was offered at the right time

It Can Happen At Any Level

We've all seen famous or powerful people who appear to have everything yet have risked it all for a quick and apparently pointless bonk. Think of Hugh Grant, adored actor who was with one of the most desirable women in the world, Elizabeth Hurley. He risked it all for a quick blowjob with a prostitute in a car in a seedy backstreet. Not to mention the famous tennis player caught in the broom cupboard of a London Japanese restaurant giving a waitress his California roll.

The world gasped with amazement that Bill Clinton, a powerful man who had the world at his fingertips, should want to use those fingertips on the average-looking Monica Lewinsky. Why would a man who seemed to have it all be so stupid as to risk the wrath of the American people in such a reckless way? By contrast, most of the famously philandering women in history are classically lonely souls searching for something they never seem to find in their relationships – Marilyn Monroe, Janis Joplin and Anna-Nicole Smith to name a few. The actions of these people make no sense at all until you look at the list of reasons people give for affairs on the previous page.

The ordinary woman lulled into playing around was perfectly illustrated by Meryl Streep in the film *The Bridges of Madison County*. She was bored and lonely, isolated by the routine dullness of her life and an apparently free spirit, played by Clint Eastwood, offered an exciting alternative. She took it and successfully hid it. But when Bill Clinton said, 'I did not have sexual relations with that woman,' and pointed his finger at the camera, you knew that he was sunk. The whole world suspected he was guilty, even if his wife still claimed blissful ignorance.

> **'Clinton lied. A man might forget where he parks or where he lives, but he never forgets oral sex, no matter how bad it is.'**
>
> *Barbara Bush (former US first lady)*

Why Women Play Around Less Than Men

The joke about men having to undo their fly to think isn't far from the truth. Most women have the planning ability to get away with murder when it comes to affairs – men don't and rarely do. Men's main problem is an inability to manage rational thought in situations dominated by sex. Most men usually don't plan an affair, it just happens. Women are much more likely to have affairs that have been on the drawing board for some time before reaching fruition. Overall, the number of women playing around is lower than the number of men, even though evidence is surfacing that shows philandering by younger women is higher than for older women. Michelle Langley, author of *Women's Infidelity*, conducted research over a ten-year period that indicates that women cheat as much as men, especially younger women. But women are by nature more nurturing and more loving than men and have lower levels of the sex-drive hormone testosterone and higher levels of the 'cuddle hormone', oxytocin, and so are less driven to have physical sex. In addition, most women go through life believing they should be the most important person in their partner's world because a woman puts her man in the number-one position in hers.

Many women will sacrifice their own needs to support their man, raise his children, run his home and be loyal to him no matter what. For a majority, this also extends to sex and the idea of being touched by or having sex with someone else is unthinkable to them. The naïve among them expect their husbands to feel the same. A training class in the differences between men and women would open the eyes of every new bride and would save a lot of marriages from divorce, which is where around 50% or more of them currently end up. The problem is that men are driven and consumed by their sex drive from the moment their hormones kick in at puberty and it lasts until the end of their days; however, as a man ages, his mind begins to make contracts that his body can't fulfil. The urge to act on it may diminish over time, but for most of his life, the male brain is very rarely off the subject.

> **Marriage has its good side. It teaches you loyalty, forbearance, tolerance, self-restraint and other valuable qualities you wouldn't need if you had stayed single.**

Six Common Myths About Cheating

Myth no. 1: it's mainly men who cheat

Baby Boomer men – born before 1962 – cheat about twice as much as Baby Boomer women, but new research shows that women in their 20s and 30s have about the same amount of affairs as men of the same age. More women in this group are working and have more financial freedom and are therefore more likely to take risks with their relationship. Around 50% of all affairs are with a person in the workplace.

Myth no. 2: there's a cheater profile

Given the right circumstances, anyone is susceptible to cheating. It's common for someone to become involved in an affair when they had no initial thoughts of being unfaithful. It may not even be consistent with a person's value system, but if the circumstances and time are right and the opportunity presents itself, they may be tempted. Perhaps a workmate makes an advance at a business conference when they're getting over a fight with their partner. Maybe they are stressed to the eyeballs and their cute gardener pays them a compliment. Yet many people believe that there's a specific type of person who's unfaithful and so they have a false sense of security. While some people are serial philanderers, affairs can happen to anyone. For men, an affair is usually opportunistic, but for women, it's usually planned. Don't fool yourself into believing you'll never have an affair. Instead, think of situations or circumstances in which you might be susceptible and make a point of avoiding them.

Myth no. 3: long-term monotony leads to an affair

More people have affairs during the first two years of marriage than at any other time. This is the time when women are asking themselves if they made the right choice or whether they would be better off with someone else. It takes at least two years of living with someone before you really know them. If a man was a serial cheater before marriage, he may also be a suspect for it during this initial period. Serial male cheaters are usually driven by a combination of higher testosterone levels and early childhood experiences, which affect how relationships are perceived as an adult.

Myth no. 4: a man is driven to infidelity when he's not happy at home

In 2007, noted infidelity researcher Shirley Glass, author of *NOT 'Just Friends'* found that people who never intended to be unfaithful unwittingly formed deep, passionate connections before they realised that they had crossed the line between platonic friendship and romantic love. For male philanderers, the opportunity just happened to appear and they really got off on the chemical highs associated with philandering. She found that women philanderers said that they had been emotionally disconnected for around a year prior to the commencement of the affair. Women also reported that the affair had been formulating in their minds for most of that time.

The bottom line is that the more emotional distance you develop between yourself and your partner, the greater the chance an affair has of starting. Open discussion about your relationship is the best way to ward off affairs.

Myth no. 5: you'll get it right second time around

Those who decide to pair up permanently with their affairees often make the decision to 'get it right this time'. The chemical changes that happen in the brain fool many cheaters into believing they will always live in 'happily-ever-after' land. Statistics show that this is the case for only 25% of those who marry their lover – 75% eventually divorce – but most who get remarried believe that they will be in the 25%. People who are having an affair live in a drug-like fantasy world, free from paying bills and cleaning the toilet. A new car always has an exciting smell to potential buyers, but after a year it still needs washing every week, requires regular servicing and feels just like a normal car.

Myth no. 6: you can usually sense when your partner is fooling around

Most people are oblivious to a straying mate for some time because they are living in their relationship based on the trust that their partner will remain faithful, so they don't look for clues. When philandering signals do become evident, some people prefer to go into denial rather than face the upset of uncovering the affair. Women are better at spotting the signals, which is why over 80% of relationships are ended by women. In *The Definitive Book of Body Language* we showed why men are not as perceptive as women, because the male brain does not have the same ability at matching the contradictory signals between speech and action. This is why so many men are shocked when they discover their women have been cheating.

The Nine Different Types of Affair

When your relationship has problems and you don't know how to fix it, you are a candidate for an affair and it may offer a temporary escape from your problems. Below are the nine types of affair that people have.

1. The Do-I-Still-Have-Market-Value? Affair

You may feel that your partner has lost interest in you or doesn't spend much time with you, or maybe you married young and feel inexperienced. Either way, you wonder what rating you might still have on the mating market. You feel a part of you is incomplete and you're resentful that your partner ignores your needs. You no longer know if you are still attractive to the opposite sex or you feel you've missed out on something. You just want to have this affair because you feel you must satisfy your self-doubts or you just want to get it out of your system. If you are in one of these affairs, once you work out your market value, you'll probably get over it. If you can contain the fallout, things usually get better at home.

2. The Mid-Life-Crisis Affair

You get to middle age and start to wonder what life is all about, what you may have missed out on and whether or not you have wasted your life. Friends your age or younger are getting illnesses or dying, and you are losing your looks as gravity takes over. Your sex drive is diminishing. The end of your life is visible on the horizon and you feel a sense of urgency to do something memorable or significant. Panic sets in and you want to do 'something crazy' to justify your existence. An affair is really not what you need – you need counselling about getting older, and you need to set new and exciting goals for your life.

3. The Comparison Affair

This is a common affair in the early years of marriage or a new permanent relationship. The person who is a candidate for this affair has nagging doubts about whether or not they made the right choice. Would they be happier with someone else, or would their current relationship problems disappear if they were with another person? If you are in this affair, you need to identify what specific aspect of your relationship you are try-ing to shine a light on and develop an action to deal with it. You don't really need an affair to do it. If you've found out what you need to know, get out of the affair and get on with real life.

4. The Time-Bomb Affair

This affair begins because you don't want to face your partner and tell them you've had enough. You're not even sure what you need or what's missing in your marriage, and you think that by blowing it up you have a chance of putting it back together in a better way. You leave clues lying around so your partner will discover the affair and this will save you from summoning up the courage to sort it out. You don't need this affair either – you need to face up to your partner and put it all on the table. This approach is less painful and less costly than the affair. A Time-Bomb Affair is seen as the easy way out, but it's not.

5. The Getting-Even Affair

Your partner has cheated on you so you have a revenge affair to even the score or to show you partner how it feels. You don't go into this affair for the emotional or sexual experience; you do it out of spite. This affair can fill you with feelings of guilt and self-loathing, and is a form of abuse, both to yourself and your affairee (unless it's a man – he'll just be grateful for the sex). If you are in this affair, remember that your goal was revenge and don't get wrapped up in the emotional side of what could be a rebounder. Get a counsellor and learn how to deal with your anger over this.

6. The Shoulder-to-Cry-On Affair

You know you're in one of these affairs when you spend more time opening up your heart to the person than having sex with them. In fact, the sex, however powerful it may be, seems almost incidental to the main benefit you are getting from the affair – free therapy. You feel understood by the other person; they support and encourage you. This is another affair you don't need – you need professional therapy. It's cheaper.

7. The Better-Offer/Upgrade Affair

This affair happens when either your market value goes up because you've got a better job, lost weight, improved your appearance, got a degree or your partner's rating has gone down because they've let themselves go or have become relationship lazy. When you got married, your partner was the best you could do at the time. Now you're older and more experienced, have a wider perspective on relationships and think you could do better. Talk to your partner about your unsettled feelings and set joint goals that will bring you both to the same market value. Whenever you upgrade anything in life, you usually pay a lot more for the new model and lose a lot on the old one. Maybe a good spring-clean and renovation of your current relationship is what is required.

8. The I-Can't-Get-My-Needs-Met Affair

Your partner refuses to do something you say you really need – be it emotional connection, talking from the heart, oral sex, anal sex, sex on a rollercoaster or anything involving AAA batteries. So you risk your entire relationship by getting it elsewhere. A good sex therapist can help you develop strategies to deal with this, or maybe you feel your unmet need is bigger than the overall relationship. In that case, you might be better to leave.

9. The Unintentional Affair

As we said earlier, given the right time, place and circumstances, almost anyone could become involved in an affair. You don't really know how you got into this affair or why, but damn, it feels good! You don't know how to end it, and you are ridden with anguish and guilt. You ask yourself, Why am I doing this? and you don't have an answer. The Unintentional Affair highlights that something was missing from your relationship and you or your partner denied it was there. Work out what it is you need and end the affair.

Why the 'Perfect Affair' Is a Fantasy

There is no such thing as an ideal affair. Keeping an affair going involves covering up lies, explaining things away and dealing with any anger or guilt. The cheater often becomes consumed by guilt and sometimes lashes out verbally or physically at their partner. If you are having an affair, respect yourself and your partner and get couples counselling or get out of the affair.

> **The relationship counsellor sent the arguing couple into the back garden to review how to best deal with their problems, where they came upon a wishing well. The wife leaned over, made a wish and threw in a coin.**
> **The husband decided to make a wish, too, but he leaned over too much, fell into the well and drowned.**
> **The wife was stunned for a moment, but then smiled and whispered to herself, 'It really works!'**

I Heard It Through the Grapevine

Suspicion that a partner is carrying on with someone else can be worse to live with than the truth. Many women will seek denial, whereas most men will generally look for proof and want to know for certain.

It's very rarely as it is on television: few people discover their partner is having an affair by walking in on them in the act – even though a large proportion of men choose their own bed in their own homes to throw the leg over. Sometimes the betrayed will hear about it through the grapevine. Friends often agonise over whether to tell someone that their partner is playing around – the fear of 'shoot-the-messenger' syndrome is very real, and some friends have other than good intentions when they spill the beans. Most women will choose to tell, fearing they too could one day be the last to know, and they believe that they would want a friend to tell them.

The most common way most people find out is written evidence. It could be a hotel bill proving the cheater to be where they should not have been, receipts for gifts or flowers that can't be explained, mobile-phone records, credit-card statements, email history or phone numbers on pieces of paper.

Eight Classic Signs of a Cheater

In the absence of hard evidence, a nosy friend or the money to pay a private detective, however, there are universal telltale signs that may suggest it is worth asking questions. Be prepared for anger at the lack of trust if your partner manages to prove your suspicions wrong, but also be prepared for the consequences if the response is the one you really don't want to hear.

> **A man came home to find his wife in bed with his best friend, so he shot his wife and gave the dog a reprieve.**

When a man or woman gets a new love interest on the side, the increased hormonal activity in the brain causes behavioural changes. These may be subtle changes to their daily habits or new habits that are designed to try to cover up normal daily routines.

Routine changes – any change in behaviours that have been part of your life as a couple can indicate a driving force outside the home: a man starts doing his own washing; an armchair TV addict joins a gym; your partner stops wearing a wedding ring or starts locking drawers...

Sex changes – there may be subtle changes in regularity or style of doing the horizontal hula, but they should not be ignored. If they want to try things they've never done with you before, there may be someone else coaching or influencing a newfound passion, sensitivity or expertise. There may also be a sudden lack of wanting to have sex at all.

Appearance changes – dieting, new clothes, showers the minute they walk in the door, him shaving twice a day, her getting a new hairstyle or cutting her hair.

Business trips – increased trips away, more than the usual number of overnighters, failure to invite you to business events, secrecy or vagueness about schedules, failure to share flight or hotel information, not being where they are supposed to be. Alternatively, they might start working late into the evening, or you may notice their workmates are uncomfortable around you.

Nervous reactions – when the phone rings or when you mention a certain person at their work. Also look out for talking in their sleep, erratic mood swings and increased criticism of you.

Conversation changes – in the case of cheating at work, someone who was mentioned in passing as part of their news of the day either figures more prominently – 'Had lunch with...' or 'Was chatting to...today' – or disappears from discussion completely. A man will often repeat the same stories, because he's forgotten who's been told what.

Technology changes – you start to notice that your partner prefers to email you rather than call you. When they call you, conversations are kept short, end abruptly or are whispered, all signs that someone else may be present. They have constant excuses to go for a walk with their mobile phone – for example, there's bad phone reception where you are sitting – or they go to the toilet too often and for too long. When you are together, they don't want to pick up certain incoming calls in your presence. They are constantly online, even when with you, checking emails, and if you approach, the window on the computer is suddenly closed. Their BlackBerry is never left lying around where you might see it. Their computer and phone suddenly have a password.

New friends – they have new work buddies you never get to meet. They call them from time to time but calls are always short: they say they'll call them back or that they don't have the information right now. If you find out that their friends are cheaters, it may be a cheaters' support group. Like attracts like.

The above clues are more often seen in men than in women. Women are more subtle in concealment, and men are generally worse when it comes to spotting clues (as detailed in *The Definitive Book of Body Language*). Often there are clues a blind dog could spot, but you would be amazed how many men will still fail to notice – for example, a complete withdrawal of her affection, suggestions that he goes away for the weekend, condoms in the travel bag, emotional distance and her preoccupation with everything but him. Women who are having an affair are likely to withdraw intimacy and sex in their marriage because duplicity comes much harder for them – most have evolved to be one-man women at heart.

For the reasons previously mentioned in this book, a man often finds his sex life at home is spiced up by a little action on the side, and because a man's brain can separate sex from love, running two or more women at one time is not difficult.

> ## Why were men given larger brains than dogs?
> ## So they won't hump women's legs at cocktail parties.

How to Handle a Cheater

The night Prince Charles gave his famous TV interview and admitted to his long-running tryst with Camilla Parker-Bowles during his marriage, Princess Diana put on her sexiest little black dress and paraded before the world at a high-profile event looking glamorous. It couldn't have been easy for her – but easier on the soul than sitting at home with a box of tissues. Men suffer less when they are betrayed, because for most the initial and lasting emotions are anger and hurt pride – these are aggressive emotions. The problem for men comes in opening up emotionally, talking to friends and communicating their hurts and fears.

As a rule, a woman will go through several distinct phases, starting with anger and hurt, but the long-term effects go much deeper. She will have a crisis of confidence and low self-esteem; she will feel more protective of her children and will feel the burden of keeping the family together as well as a lack of options. She is also likely to feel responsible in some way for the fact that her partner fancied another woman. The most common side effects for betrayed women are depression and physical illness because high stress levels deplete the immune system and leave the body unguarded against infection and disease. She will catch everything going from her kids' head colds to joint and back pain caused by the rigid tension gripping her body day and night.

Many women will blame the other woman for their partner's infidelity, which is part of the denial syndrome. They can't believe that the man they love and have built their lives around could hurt and let them down like this. Often women decide to stay after a series of his one-night stands; many even stay after his extended affairs, which they are promised will end; and some even stay for years through a succession of quick bonks and long-running mistresses.

> **Some people think the grass is always greener on the other side of the fence. It's true – that's where the sewer pipe runs.**

They do it for several reasons: they love him; they love their kids; they love family life and the social standing of being a couple with children. Importantly, they don't want to lose their resources – their house and income. Their self-esteem sinks so low they can't imagine anyone else ever loving them, so some women decide that a man's playing around is a trade-off for a nice house, income and lifestyle – in other words, she'll hang around for the resources. But a woman who decides to hang in there may do so at great emotional and physical cost to herself, and there are no guarantees he will not leave anyhow. Having said that, it's rare that a man will leave a relationship because he's unhappy. He will stay in a relationship simply because he hasn't got a better offer. One-night stands can turn into romantic love or long-term attachment, if he decides that the new woman is worth the agony of leaving his current relationship.

A man who stays after discovering his wife's affair is more likely to do so if the affair was kept quiet and no one knew about it. Male pride gets severely damaged by a woman's affair. Public knowledge of it makes him look and feel bad, and his primal self tells him that his paternity is no longer guaranteed. As we said, unless a man has a better offer on the horizon, he's more likely to stay and try to work things out – unless she decides to kick him out.

The reality of coping with life after the decision to stay can be tougher than jumping ship and starting again. Very few people manage to find an outlet for pent-up hurt and aggression while trying to hide the hurt and deny to themselves that their partner is a cheat. The right outlet for anger and hurt is the person who has caused it – their partner – not the person with whom they had the affair.

> **'You have two choices in life:**
> **you can stay single and be miserable**
> **or get married and wish you were dead.'**
>
> *Bob Hope*

Those who confront their cheating partner also suffer feelings of self-loathing for allowing themselves to be reduced to the level of many scorned lovers – screaming in the street, fighting, smashing cars, throwing bricks through windows, posting Internet revenge blogs or cutting the arms off clothes.

Some men and women see revenge affairs as their only option, but these can seriously backfire. After an initial ego-boost, they may get dumped and be left feeling used and abused again. Besides, a revenge affair only puts them down to the same level as the one who betrayed them.

Getting Things Right

A serial cheater is not good marriage material and needs personal counselling and re-evaluation if they are ever to sustain a long-term relationship of any value. Their partner is better off starting again rather than attempting to make a happy life with a serial philanderer. You wouldn't intentionally look for a criminal or con-artist for a partner, so why chase a serial cheater?

The person having a long-term affair must be forced to choose. There is no real future – other than one of illness and depression – for anyone who chooses to stay while their partner continually cheats. If the situation continues unresolved, it can only end in misery and a high emotional price will be paid by all.

The biggest challenge for those who want to resolve their problems and resurrect their relationship is to leave the wreckage behind and build a better new relationship with their partner than the one they previously had.

A Guide to Recovery After an Affair

1 **Communicate.** Unless you talk about what happened, why and how it happened, you will never find a way of moving on. Be honest and don't be afraid to ask a question even if you don't like the answer. Only these answers can unlock the key to the future.

2 **Speak openly.** If you had the affair, admit that it was a mistake and state that you genuinely want to save your relationship. You may be afraid of the consequences, but

the confession will give you a much greater chance of putting things right than if your partner hears about it some other way. Be heartened by the fact the revelation of an affair can often be all that you need to restart your ailing marriage, because it often provides the shock necessary to make people stop, reassess and improve.

3 **Avoid blaming each other** for what you did or didn't do. It is a negative approach and won't help you uncover and address the problems that led to the affair.

4 **Don't make hasty decisions.** Allow time for the shock to pass. This will allow you to make an informed, logical assessment of the situation. After a week or so, you will feel calmer and able to make major decisions about the future of your relationship.

5 **Accept a period of mourning.** The relationship as you knew it is gone and will never return. Putting on a 'normal' face to the world does not mean you can convince yourself that everything will carry on as it was before.

6 **If you can't say it, write it down.** This has proved very useful for men who find difficulty in communicating their feelings and fears. Talking is not one of men's strong points, so don't have endless post-mortems about the affair. Stick to the point.

7 **Make a list.** You and your partner should make a list of what needs to change or receive attention to set the relationship right. It's amazing how the things that appear on people's lists are often simple and straightforward. It's a wonder why they weren't spotted as flashpoints before the affair, but the problem is things get buried beneath the avalanche of daily family life.

8 **Be kind to yourselves.** Give yourselves a leave of absence from chores that do not really need to be done, or done as often, if they encroach on quality time spent together making each other feel good.

9 **Work on your self-esteem together.** Following an affair, the only salvageable marriage is one that includes a

healthy level of remorse on both sides, but don't allow it to overwhelm you. Try to turn it into a positive conclusion. The best way to rid yourself of guilt is to accept your part in the mess and banish it for good by putting things right.

Four Vital Strategies to Avoid Becoming a Cheater Yourself

1 **Always make your partner your number-one priority.** Relationships in which one or both partners have their main focus on careers, business or children are at high risk of an affair. While these things are important, never let them always be number one in your life.

2 **Have confidences that only you and your partner talk about.** Don't share private or intimate thoughts with others that you haven't discussed with your mate.

3 **Connect with each other on a daily basis.** Couples who make time to discuss their thoughts with their partners every day have the least incidence of infidelity and the highest sense of security.

4 **Avoid any situations that allow affairs to happen.** Avoid any circumstances in which you may become temporarily attracted to someone else. This doesn't mean there's a problem in your relationship or that you have to act on it; it simply means you need to stay away from these situations.

Summary

Infidelity is the thing any person in a relationship most fears, but there are almost always warning signals when one partner is unhappy and likely to stray. By talking and communicating your feelings and fears to your partner and keeping in touch with the heart of the relationship, you can build a barrier to keep infidelity out.

Affairs rarely solve problems; they always create new ones.

> ## 'A man who marries his mistress leaves a vacancy in that position.'
> *Oscar Wilde*

A new person brings new demands, and the bigger the age difference, the more complicated those problems will be. Most cheaters confuse lust and the 'fear-of-discovery' ingredient with love. An affair is a completely selfish, one-on-one time with someone with no discussion about the realities of real life – who will scrub the toilet, who'll drive the kids to piano lessons or take out the rubbish. Even if a person marries their affairee, most of the lust hormones that drove them together disappear for 90% of people after 12–24 months, when the thrill of discovery is gone and life becomes routine once again.

Those caught in an affair stand to lose 50% or more of their social contacts with divorce, the same amount or more of their resources, and they must juggle the relationships between their new love and any existing kids, brothers, sisters, parents, their ex and work colleagues, some of whom will reject their new partner.

Relate, the UK's leading relationship organisation, found that 50% of couples who ended a long-term relationship later regretted that decision. An affair does not have to spell the end of a relationship but can also be a wake-up call that a problem exists and that one or both partners were in denial. When a man or woman is unfaithful, it is because the relationship needs to change in some way.

Regular relationship counselling can head off the majority of problems that lead to affairs.

- Affairs can happen to anyone, in any relationship.
- Affairs don't solve problems; they simply create new ones.
- Tackle problems head-on with couples counselling.

Chapter 7
How to Find the Right Partner(s) – the Mating Rating Quiz

BASED ON YOUR PERSONAL DATA FILE MR PHILSTEIN, HERE'S THE FIRST PICTURE OF YOUR PERFECT PARTNER...

'I decided to marry her. Courtship would be a mere formality. But what could I say to begin the courtship? "Would you like some chewing gum?" seemed too low-class. "Hey, babe" was too trite a greeting for my future bride. "I love you! I am hot with passion!" was too forward. "I want to make you the mother of my children" seemed a bit premature. So I said nothing. That's right – nothing. I just sat there and did nothing. After a while, the bus reached her stop, she got off, and I never saw her again.'

How Most Relationships Start

For most of us, relationships begin by accident. While an increasing number of people meet through dating agencies and the Internet, about half of us bump into potential partners through the course of our work, and the rest meet accidentally at clubs, pubs, bars, discos, barbeques and on blind dates. Most of us meet our partner by accident without any planning or clear goal-setting, yet we wonder why divorce rates are so high.

If you were the HR manager of a company and you were hiring a top-level senior executive, you'd insist on a CV, health report, financial statement, bankruptcy and credit check, and you'd want references from previous employers. If they had been in jail or were a mass murderer, you'd want to know, right? So why would you entertain a new relationship with someone you've just met in a club or pub and about whom you know nothing? Well, that's exactly how most of us get started with our partners – by accident. During the first year or so of a new relationship, people work at minimising their negatives and highlighting their positives and so for a long time they don't really find out who that person is.

The perfect person for you is the one you have **absolutely no doubts that you definitely, positively, absolutely want in your life for ever.** There's no hurry. Age is no longer a major issue, and there are plenty of people available for you.

Every relationship you have is a learning exercise and a stepping stone to the ideal partner for you.

When it comes to choosing a long-term partner, good judgement is far more helpful than emotions and feelings. As we have said, early love is based on a combination of brain chemicals that are designed to propel you into reproduction with little or no consideration for whether someone is suitable for you. Any life-changing decision you make about a partner should be carefully structured if you and they are to be a good match. A bad match can have serious consequences and make your life miserable. The most intelligent way to approach finding a life partner is in a similar way you would handle a high-profile job interview. Why let a complete stranger change your life and change it because you've experienced an overdose of hormones?

Matching With the Right Partner

Finding the right partner is entirely dependent on two things:

1 Knowing exactly what you want in a partner.
2 Being able to give what they want in return.

As you have now discovered, ancestral women wanted resources in men. Consequently, men have evolved to be accumulators of resources, gain power or both. Ancestral men sought reproductive ability in women, thus women have evolved with the motivation to do whatever is necessary to appear young, healthy and fertile. Consciously or subconsciously, men and women understand what the opposite sex wants. Just as a fisherman baits his hook to attract a fish, so men and women do what is necessary to attract a potential mate.

> **Women bait men with the offer of sex;**
> **men bait women with the offer of resources.**

It's here that current generations of young people have become confused. Young women have been brainwashed into believing that because men and women are supposedly now the same – that is, 'equal' – today's men now want extended romantic encounters with long bouts of courtship, foreplay, discussions about feelings and game-playing. The truth is that the men of the 21st century are hardwired to want exactly what their forefathers wanted: as much sex as possible with plenty of variety – and as soon as possible.

Experienced men who understand women's basic needs will participate in the romance and courtship routines to get what they want, but the higher the status of the man, the less time he's prepared to invest in doing it. While Brad Pitt could probably bed an attractive woman in less than 30 minutes, it could take Joe in accounts at the local bank 6 months of courtship rituals to bed her.

Core Values and Beliefs

While a man's resources and a woman's health and youth are the initial hardwired motivators for human attraction, all studies into what makes lasting relationships have come to the same conclusion – those that endure do so because they have the same or similar core values and beliefs.

Couples who last have the same or similar core values and beliefs.

Core values are:

1 Attitude to raising children and to discipline
2 The division of domestic chores and responsibilities
3 Finances – what, where and how money is spent
4 Cleanliness and living standards
5 Social and family – involvement, activities and frequency
6 Sex and intimacy – who needs what and will it be given?

Core beliefs are:

1 Spiritual and religious
2 Ethical and moral
3 Political and cultural

There is no such thing as a compatible couple. Most couples disagree about the same things: money, sex, kids and time. A successful long-term relationship is about having chemistry, similar core values and beliefs, and about how you manage your differences. You create compatibility. Remember that after one to two years, the rush of love hormones subsides for most people and it is similar core values and beliefs that keep couples together. When you meet someone new, they will usually be on their best behaviour for about a year, so it takes time to find out what someone's core values or beliefs really are.

Here are three simple questions to test Mr or Ms Right's potential in the early stages of a new relationship:

1. **What are their base values?** How does the person treat others, such as friends, relatives and co-workers? Are they caring, attentive, loving and affectionate? How someone treats a dog or how they deal with a waiter in a restaurant is how they will eventually treat you.
2. **What do their actions say?** A person can tell you anything, but their actions reveal the real person. If they say you're the only one for them but they spend more time with their friends, their actions reveal the truth.
3. **What do your friends think?** While your own opinion is the ultimate one, close friends can see things that a hormonally charged, besotted lover is blind to. Friends can help you to be objective about the reality.

The Five Most Common 'New-Relationship' Mistakes

Most people will identify with what is written here because most of us have made these partner misjudgements at some time in our lives.

Mistake no. 1: making hormonal choices

When someone falls 'madly in love', they make decisions

based on their feelings at the time, not on the suitability of a potential long-term mate. As discussed in Chapter 1, in the lust/romantic love stages, the brain is flooded with hormones, creating a drug-like state. If you feel you are about to commit yourself to a person because they 'have something magnetic about them…a magical feeling you just can't describe', take a cold shower and read Chapter 1 again. It's your hormones talking to you, not your brain. Sure, go for the fun of the ride of exciting new love, but decide in advance that whoever you may fall for you'll let time pass before you make any decisions about the future.

Mistake no. 2: denial of problems

You may deny to yourself that the person has problems that you may have knowledge of or refuse to listen to others about flaws your lover may have. You may focus on their positive points and see them only as you want them to appear. Any information you receive about the person should be used to make an intelligent, considered choice.

Mistake no. 3: choosing needy people

You attract someone who pleads that they need you and you spend your time 'being there' for them and constantly trying to fix their neuroses. Eventually, you'll become tired of this and will look for someone else. Alternatively, if you are the needy one because you've just been dumped, divorced or separated, you become a candidate for being a rebounder. Give yourself time – 10% of your previous relationship time – to get through the bereavement period. Then find someone who wants to be with you, not needs to be with you.

Mistake no. 4: being compliant

You spend your time desperately avoiding any disagreement

with your new love, trying to make them happy and avoiding doing or saying anything that might upset them. You become a 'yes-person', but no one respects a yes-person. By being passive and compliant, you soon build anger and resentment in yourself and it teaches your partner that you either have no real feelings or that your feelings don't count for anything. Consequently, you leave yourself open to emotional abuse. You need at least two to three good arguments or fights with your new love before you can get a realistic handle on how they really are.

Mistake no. 5: picking a partner who you think you can change

'I know he's had a bad history with relationships, but when he's with me, he'll be different. He'll change.' Ahh...no, he won't. People who believe they can change a person or that someone will be different with them are always asking for a tough life. Many women believe that the magical power of love will recreate a new man before their very eyes, but what normally happens is that their new lover simply re-establishes their past bad habits in the new relationship. It normally doesn't happen until much later in the relationship because in the early stages of romantic love, most people show their best side and hide their bad habits.

The median length of a marriage in 2007 was 12 years.

The Mating Rating

Every person has a rating number, known as their Mating Rating, and it's usually a number between zero and ten. It's a measure of how desirable each of us is on the mating market at any time. We all rate others consciously or unconsciously using this measure, and we do it to every person we see or meet. The rating is based on the desired characteristics men and women want in a partner.

When we look at a couple sitting in a restaurant or walking past us, we rate both sexes out of ten and decide if they are an equal couple. We assess whether it is a mutually beneficial relationship and whether or not they could be getting what they want from the relationship – that is, do they look like they fit? We evaluate their presentation, attractiveness, body shape, symmetry, resources, beauty and so on.

For example, super-mates Brad Pitt and Angelina Jolie would both rate a ten for many people because they seem to have it all – money, fame, power and attractiveness. They have the same Mating Rating. Yet with some other couples you shake your head and fail to see what she sees in him and vice versa – or how the relationship even works. You think, He can do much better, or, She must be desperate.

If you get the opportunity to talk to the couple and get to know them better, you will then either increase or decrease their rating. If they are rich, funny, kind or intelligent, you increase their Mating Rating, whereas if they are mean, calculating, boring or broke, you decrease their Mating Rating.

> **'Penguins mate for life. Which doesn't really surprise me because they all look exactly alike. It's not like they're gonna meet a better-looking penguin someday.'**
>
> *Ellen DeGeneres*

All studies into human mating agree that each of us has the best chance of a successful long-term relationship with someone who has the *same Mating Rating* as us. Someone who is a seven, for example, has the best long-term chance with a partner who is also a seven. They may fantasise about Kylie Minogue or Brad Pitt but will usually end up with a mate just like themselves, and if that mate's core values and beliefs are consistent with theirs and there's chemistry as well, you've probably got a perfect match. Relationship problems happen when one partner's mating rating significantly changes. For example, the man increases his resources by getting a big promotion or winning the lottery and moves from a 7 to an 8.5, or the woman decreases her rating through self-neglect or becomes overweight and decreases to, say, a 5. He then becomes critical of her, while she starts to overcompensate with her performance to try to make up the gap.

The Mating Rating Quiz –
How Do You Measure Up
In the Market Place?

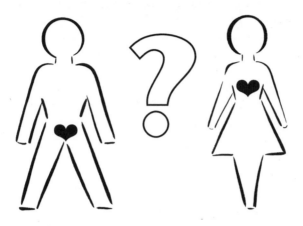

This quiz has been designed to evaluate your Mating Rating – that is, where people of the opposite sex (or those who have the opposite brain wiring to you) see you on the Desirability Scale. This quiz is good for anyone who wants to improve their Mating Rating and jump up to the next level. It will help you to pinpoint your weaker areas and the areas in which you are not achieving. No matter which category you achieve in this test, if you are happy to be in that category, then that's OK. If you are not happy in a category, however, this test will guide you to the areas in which you'll need improvement. We have found that people are usually tough on themselves and we suggest that you ask someone who knows you well to do the quiz with you to guide you towards what they think could be the most accurate response for you. This way, you will discover not only how you see yourself but how others see you. Many people will be surprised at how others see them compared to how they rate themselves.

Answer all the questions before looking at the scoring system so that you stay honest with yourself.

Male quiz

Section 1	RARELY	SOMETIMES	MOSTLY
1. I am within my recommended Body Mass Index.			
2. I tell the truth on my résumé.			
3. If a woman made flirtatious eye contact with me in a bar, I would recognise the signals.			
4. I can read between the lines of what people say.			
5. I do regular exercise and/or sport.			
6. I take credit for things that I do, not what I haven't done.			
7. When I see a special or unique gift, I often buy it for someone.			
8. I have a V-shaped upper body.			
9. When I am in a relationship, I handwrite notes and send texts and emails telling my partner how special she is.			
10. Most people think I have a good sense of humour.			
11. I love children and animals.			
12. I know what the G-spot is and how to find it.			
13. I am a good listener and am compassionate to others' needs.			
14. People who know me would say I have good manners.			
15. I have good skin and a clear complexion.			
16. What is your height compared to the average man?	SHORTER	AVERAGE	TALLER
Total of ticks in each column			

Section 2	RARELY	SOMETIMES	MOSTLY
17. I like to meet new people, make new friends and am approachable.			
18. I can laugh at myself.			
19. I can sense when others feel pain, hurt and sorrow.			
20. I update my wardrobe regularly – especially underwear.			
21. I often think about ways I can make my partner feel loved.			
22. I can easily laugh about daily life and I laugh readily.			
23. People who know me would say I have good common sense.			
24. I take into consideration the needs of significant people in my life.			
25. I take pride in my personal grooming – for example, my hair, nails and skin are clean.			
26. I enjoy jokes and laugh at them.			
27. When I meet someone who I would like to have a relationship with and who has an interest in me, I do everything I can to court them.			
28. I regularly say, 'I love you,' to my partner.			
29. I often make dinner, wash the dishes or give my partner the night off.			
30. Most people think I am an honest, upstanding individual.			
31. I am confident in my physical appearance and physical abilities.			
32. When life is tough, I can still find something to be positive about.			
33. When I decide to accomplish something, I see it through to the end.			

34.	If someone drops £20, I pick it up and give it to them.			
35.	People who know me would say I am street-smart.			
36.	My body is symmetrical. (One side matches the other.)	NO	FAIRLY	YES
	Total of ticks in each column			

	Section 3	RARELY	SOMETIMES	MOSTLY
37.	I have a positive attitude to life and clear goals. I am ambitious.			
38.	I am willing to share my resources with the partner in my life.			
39.	I know that first impressions are critical to how well I get on.			
40.	I strive to increase my resources.			
41.	The way I groom and dress myself can influence my status with others.			
42.	I would never keep secrets from my partner and believe honesty is the best way.			
43.	If an obstacle appears in my life, I can find creative solutions to rectify it.			
44.	I strive to improve my skills.			
45.	With your palm facing towards you, look at the ring finger on your hand. Is it longer or shorter than your index finger?	SHORTER	THE SAME	LONGER
46.	What are your income and assets compared to the average man?	LOWER	AVERAGE	HIGHER
	Total of ticks in each column			

Total score

Section 1	RARELY	SOMETIMES	MOSTLY
Total ticks in each column			
Multiply by	1	2	3
Section 1 Total			

Section 2	RARELY	SOMETIMES	MOSTLY
Total ticks in each column			
Multiply by	1	4	6
Section 2 Total			

Section 3	RARELY	SOMETIMES	MOSTLY
Total ticks in each column			
Multiply by	1	6	9
Section 3 Total	RARELY	SOMETIMES	MOSTLY

Enter in each Section Total to give your Overall Total

COMBINE YOUR SCORES = OVERALL TOTAL = YOUR MATING RATING

Female quiz

Section 1	RARELY	SOMETIMES	MOSTLY
1. If an obstacle appears in my life, I can find creative solutions to rectify it.		✓	
2. I can laugh at myself.		✓	
3. I am within my recommended Body Mass Index.			✓
4. I can find lots to laugh about in daily life and I laugh readily.		✓	
5. I am a good listener.			✓
6. When life is tough, I can still find something to laugh about.	✓		
7. I enjoy and laugh at jokes men tell.		✓	
8. I do regular exercise and/or sport.		✓	
9. I pay attention and listen without jumping to conclusions.		✓	
10. People who know me would say I am street-smart.	✓		
11. I stay focused on getting a job done.		✓	
12. When I'm with a group of very successful people, I feel comfortable speaking with them.			✓
13. Most people I know think I have a good sense of humour.		✓	
14. People who know me would say I have good common sense.			✓
15. What is your height compared to the average woman?	TALLER	AVERAGE	SHORTER ✓
Total of ticks in each column	2	8	5

Section 2	RARELY	SOMETIMES	MOSTLY
16. I like to meet new people and make new friends.		✓	
17. I have clear skin and a good complexion.			✓
18. I make my partner number one when there are other men around.		✓	
19. I am easy to approach and I talk to others freely.	✓		
20. I have good hygiene/grooming.			✓
21. I keep details about past lovers and relationships confidential.			✓
22. Men's desire for pornography does not bother me.		✓	
23. I have a positive attitude to life.		✓	
24. I take pride in my appearance and take action when I am unhappy with it.			✓
25. I take my time before deciding to have sex with a new partner.			✓
26. I know how to make a man feel intelligent and important.			✓
27. My face is symmetrical. (One side matches the other.)	NO	FAIRLY	YES ✓
Total of ticks in each column	1	4	7

Section 3	RARELY	SOMETIMES	MOSTLY
28. Fidelity to my partner is important to me.			✓
29. I have orgasms.		✓	
30. I have at least one set of sexy lingerie.		✓	
31. I am creative about sex and I initiate it.	✓		
32. I have a hips-to-waist ratio of about 70%.		✓	

	LONGER	THE SAME	SHORTER
33. With your palm facing towards you, look at the ring finger on your hand. Is it longer or shorter than your index finger?			✓

	OLDER	AVERAGE	YOUNGER
34. Do you look older or younger than your actual age?			✓
Total of ticks in each column	1	3	3

Total score

Section 1	RARELY	SOMETIMES	MOSTLY
Total ticks in each column	2	8	5
Multiply by	1	2	3
Section 1 Total (33)	2	16	15

Section 2	RARELY	SOMETIMES	MOSTLY
Total ticks in each column	1	4	7
Multiply by	1	4	6
Section 2 Total (59)	1	16	42

Section 3	RARELY	SOMETIMES	MOSTLY
Total ticks in each column	1	3	3
Multiply by	1	6	9
Section 3 Total (46)	RARELY	SOMETIMES	MOSTLY
	1	18	27

Enter in each Section Total to give your Overall Total

COMBINE YOUR SCORES = OVERALL TOTAL = YOUR MATING RATING (138)

Scoring and results

Male scores: 46–109
Female scores: 34–77

This is the group with the lowest desirability rating. This group, however, also has the greatest chance of improvement in their Mating Rating – the only way is up! People at the lower end of this spectrum don't care much about their appearance, their status, their ability to earn resources, their health or their general well-being.

People in this group will source people in the same group and will feel happy with their lot in life – their potential partners won't see any need to change and probably won't be reading this book anyway.

Someone with a rating at the higher end of this spectrum is more likely to be reading this book and be prepared to move their Mating Rating up because they want to make changes in their life.

Those who scored in this group have the opportunity to increase their Mating Rating by improving the areas in which they scored low. They can take a course, read books, join a gym, attend seminars and so on. These people need more belief and encouragement to improve themselves, and by tackling one area at a time, they can stay focused and improve.

Male scores: 110–215
Female scores: 78–150

This group of people can tend to slip backwards or forwards. They can drop to the lower end but with hard work they can also move quickly up the scale. The highest percentage of the human population is in this group.

Many people will be happy to stay in this range because most possible partners also fall into this category. To go to the next level needs hard work, but if they want to go there, they can. Higher-quality partners are on the higher levels.

If someone in this category doesn't like the way they look,

they can hire a personal trainer, attend seminars, read books, book a stylist, improve their health, join Toastmasters or a community club or association; they can participate in community-based projects, attend training courses, hire a mentor or get a life coach. This work not only spills over in their personal life but into their business life, which will increase income and success potential.

Male scores: 216–58
Female scores: 151–80

The people in this range are confident, self-assured go-getters. They know what they want in life and they regularly go for it. Rarely will this bracket drop down a level unless there is a major crisis that drags them down, but before long they will be planning to get back up there. If this group has a problem, they don't need to be told; they are probably already doing something about it. These people are resourceful. This is where movie stars, millionaires, world leaders, CEOs, business leaders and the most desirable partners live.

Summary

Wherever you are on the Mating Rating Desirability Scale, it is not a fixed position. You can improve your rating by setting goals to improve your desirability and by taking positive action. Being desirable to others is more about your attitude, how you think and what you are doing with yourself and your life than what you were born with. If you decide, you can move yourself to almost any level of desirability and dramatically increase the number of quality partners who will become available to you. Many people are happy to stay exactly where they currently are on the Desirability Scale, but remember that you will only ever attract a long-term partner who has the same Mating Rating as you. If you want better partners, however, reread your answers to this quiz and you will know what to do next.

How to Find a Great Partner

In 2009, the world's population was 6.744 billion, of which 50.5% were male and 49.5% were female; 3.8 billion of these were aged 18–60. Assuming that 80% of these are in the worst Third World countries, in jail, insane or generally unavailable, there are 380 million normal people who are the opposite sex to you. It is estimated that around 1 in 50 of the opposite sex has the right chemistry for you – that's 7.6 million people who can make your heart beat, on sight. Assuming that 1 in 5 of this group has similar core values and beliefs to you, there are at least 1.52 million perfect partners somewhere out there waiting to meet you.

Finding a perfect partner is like selling – it's a numbers game, and the more prospects you see, the greater the chance you have of finding a sale. In sales, a typical ratio for a product that sells for $1,000 is **5:4:3:1**. This means for every:

5 prospects a salesperson has
4 is the number they actually see
3 listen to their presentation
1 says, 'Yes.'

The world's top salespeople don't spend their lives looking for the one person who is a buyer; they look instead for groups of five prospects to call on. When you use this 'averages' approach, the buyers will simply appear. So the salesperson's success is determined by how often they call on five new prospects, not how many people buy. And so it is for successful lovers. They don't sit at home waiting to be discovered; they get active and see as many prospects as they can. Put simply, be as socially active as possible. As demonstrated, there are over 1.52 million potentially perfect prospects somewhere in the world for you, but right now they don't know you exist. You have to find them.

You'll rarely find Mr or Ms Right in a pub or a nightclub, because that's where people go for casual mates, not for long-term relationships.

Choose something you'd like to learn – for example, scuba-diving – then join a club and go on weekend trips. You'll learn a skill and meet lots of new people. Take a course in something that you have been interested in for a long time but haven't started. You could learn to paint, dance, take photographs or start up any other interest that you would love to try. You will meet people with whom you have an immediate rapport because they like similar things to you. This way, there is a greater chance they may also have similar core values and beliefs to you. You'll also make new friends of the same sex, who can be a great avenue for you to meet their single friends.

Like selling, finding partners is all about the numbers game.

Never join a club just to find a partner – but don't limit your prospecting. The bottom line is that you make a plan and stick to it. The harder you work for it, the more likely you will be to find your ideal partner.

How to Change Your Love Life For Ever

We are now going to ask you to take control of your love life and stop letting relationships happen by accident. What you are about to read can change your life for ever. Have you ever written a list of goals that you thought you wanted to achieve? You'll probably answer 'Yes' for your work life because businesses can't survive without written goals and targets. If you have written goals, you'll know that the pathway to these goals suddenly materialises. When you decide to buy a certain type of car – say, a blue Toyota sedan – as soon as you decided exactly what you wanted, you started to see blue Toyota sedans everywhere, right? Here's how it works – you can take in and absorb less than 5% of what happens around you, otherwise your brain would become overwhelmed by too much information and it couldn't cope. So your brain actively searches only for data related to the things you have in your mind and ignores the rest. Anytime you make a decision to do something or to achieve anything, you immediately begin to see things about it in newspapers, on TV, in magazines and you'll hear it in people's conversations. It's like when you've read the newspaper and would swear you've read everything and someone asks, 'Did you see the story about…?' and you can't recall seeing it. You return to the newspaper and find an entire page devoted to the story. The story wasn't part of your priority list, so your brain didn't see it.

Now we want you to write a list of the characteristics and attributes of your perfect life partner. Don't compromise. Why should you compromise when there are over a million potential outstanding partners out there somewhere for you? You must also be realistic – there's no point in writing that you want Brad Pitt or Elle Macpherson unless you're prepared to upscale yourself to the level that they would want in a partner. Part of the reason love evolved was to help us fall for someone whose attractiveness, intelligence, status and overall Mating Rating are similar to ours, as this would help us avoid chasing someone who is unattainable. We promise you this – whatever you write down on your list will immediately begin to appear around you and be drawn to you. And it does not fail.

How Robert approached it

As an example, here's a list that Robert, one of our male readers, wrote at one of our seminars:

Tall, blue-eyed, blonde hair
Athletic, trim and is into fitness
Has a good sense of humour
Is daring and will push boundaries
Is not materialistic about life
Would be a caring parent
Will always make me number one
Is a whore in the bedroom

For Robert, this woman would be his perfect mate. When Robert first wrote this list, he felt a little uncomfortable about doing it but was prepared to give it a go. He'd always written detailed goal lists for business but never for a life partner (which is why he'd gone from one bad relationship to the next). He later reported that when he had completed his 'perfection' list, he started seeing women who matched his criteria everywhere, just as he had described his ideal woman on his list – and just as it had happened with his blue Toyota sedan. He carried his list with him for over two years and repeatedly had dates with women who matched his criteria. We know that if he'd never written this list that day, he may never have found the blue-eyed blonde he has now been ecstatically married to for the past six years.

'I was standing at the counter of a coffee lounge when Fiona walked in,' he said. 'My heart stopped when I saw her, and when she spoke, I felt paralysed. I reached into my pocket and pulled out my list. She was the woman on my list! She took the coffee and sat at a table. I approached her with my heart in my mouth and said, "Do you mind if I join you for a few minutes? I'd like to ask your advice." She said, "Sure," and that's how it started. I had no idea what to say because I'd never done this before. I explained that I'd been to a seminar where we were asked to write a list of our ideal life partner. I asked her to comment on my list. Fortunately, I'd changed the last item from "whore in the bedroom" to "tiger in the bedroom" in case I met my match and showed her my list. Fiona was both stunned and flattered. If I had never written the list and had it with me on that day, I would never have had the courage to make that approach. Fiona would have just walked into my life and then walked out again!'

> **'My mother said it was simple to keep a man...A woman needs to be a maid in the living room, a cook in the kitchen and a whore in the bedroom.'**
>
> *Jerry Hall*

If your list said you wanted a redheaded, green-eyed person with freckles, that's who you'd begin to see around you. The list idea works. Do it now and stop being a member of the 'accidental-relationship' club. If you meet a wonderful partner by accident, it's a bonus, but don't let chance be your only relationship plan.

What Susan wanted

Another delegate, Susan, wrote the following 'wish list' of her ideal partner's attributes:

Tall
Slim build
Dark hair
Hazel eyes
Athletic
Loves the outdoors
Business executive
Loves children
Pet lover
Non-smoker
Romantic
Ambitious

Susan put this list on her refrigerator and carried another with her in her purse. She looked at it regularly. Like most goal-setting, you should not only write it down and refer to it regularly, you should tell your friends and they'll start to see this person appear, too. The list technique will save you time and heart-break because you'll know exactly who you are looking for, and if someone walks into your life who doesn't match your list, you won't waste your time or hope they'll change. If a person has at least, say, 70% of your requirements and you feel you could live with what they don't have, then spend the time getting to know them better. But if they only have 20% of the qualities you are looking for, forget it. Susan has reported that since writing her list, she has been amazed to see men who match this description literally jump out everywhere, including at supermarkets, in the gym, on TV and crossing the road at traffic lights. Her brain is programmed to search for the things in a partner that are important to her. That's why this idea works.

Your list needs to describe your minimum requirements for a permanent partner. If a prospective partner doesn't qualify for most or all your written criteria, look elsewhere.

How to Play the Numbers Game With Your List

Graham Steele, author of *All the Best Ones Aren't Taken*, was an expert at playing the ratios and numbers game in sales and business. When he became newly single at age 50, he decided to apply the numbers formula to the thousands of dating sites on the Internet to find his ideal partner.

His results were so dramatic he wrote a book about what happened – and he met the love of his life. In 2009, we inter-viewed Graham about how he had applied the numbers game to the mating market and here is what he said: 'First, I wrote a description of exactly who I was looking for. I had been mar-ried previously, I'd had a number of relationships that didn't work out and so I decided I would find my perfect partner, and never settle for second best.'

This is what he wrote on his list as his perfect female partner:

Age 25–45
Well presented
Fit and healthy
Caring, loving and attentive
Non-smoker
University degree
Loves music, musician
Articulate and cultured

'After I wrote this list, I then wrote a description of myself, trying to be as honest as I could and not exaggerating anything. Next, I chose a good photograph of myself and began posting the details on matchmaking websites around the world. Soon it became almost a full-time job managing the responses, but if I was going to get the result I wanted, I would do it. I soon averaged sixty hours a week online for close to three years, posting my details, answering the responses and chatting to women on my computer. I met a lot of weirdos, some real crazy people, and I had a lot of fun.'

Here's a summary of what Graham did:

1. He looked at over 20,000 headshots and descriptions on dating websites.
2. He got it down to around 1,000 women's photos and full descriptions of themselves. That's about 5% of the total women he had sifted through.
3. He sent his photo and description to these 1,000 women and 30% responded (about 300).
4. In a return email, he asked them if they wanted to have children – most said, 'Yes' – about 285.
5. Next, he responded to this 285 with the 'kill factor' – stating clearly that he was not going to have any more kids, as he already had three. About 60% dropped out.
6. This left him with about 100 women with whom he could develop a relationship. That's 10% of the 1,000

women he thought were suitable candidates.

7.   With each of these 100 women they learned about each other over time through Internet chat, phone calls and emails, 38 came to meet him, and these relationships either strengthened or died.

8.   From this 100 women, he invited 24 from foreign countries to holiday with him in Brisbane, Australia, on the basis that they paid their airfares and he would pay for everything else; 16 accepted.

9.   Those who accepted also accepted the concept of pre-marital sex, so that if chemistry happened, they could both fully evaluate each other's partner potential.

10. Women came from everywhere (including the 16 from overseas), and mostly, they had a great time. Some arrived as virgins and left the same way – 'my choice'. If there was no chemistry with them, he considered it a waste of time.

'Of all the women I met, Emma stood out in every respect even before I met her face to face. I remember clearly the day Emma contacted me – it was Easter Monday and I had spent eight hours studying women on Match.com and had responded to a hundred of them *that day*. Eventually, three of that group came to see me in Brisbane, and one was close to my ideal, except that she sulked and seemed like she'd be hard work. But Emma was absolutely perfect. When she arrived in Australia, we instantly felt the chemistry. We soon became engaged and were married the following year. That was nine years ago.' When Graham met Emma, he was a 50-year-old property developer, guitarist and singer. Emma was a 29-year-old Chinese woman who held an accounting degree and fitted Graham's list perfectly. She was also a guitar player who has since learned to play classical piano. When we interviewed Graham and Emma, they had been together and happily married for nine years and are two people we would describe as perfectly matched for a life together.

We asked Emma how she felt about being the result of what could be considered by some as a massive relationship lottery. 'Graham chose me to be his wife from a possible twenty thousand other women,' she said. 'How many women can claim that of any man? I have no doubt that I am number one in Graham's life.'

'Emma is the woman I always wanted,' said Graham. 'Most people don't have a big enough pool of partners to choose from – that's why they can't afford to be as choosy as I was. You need a written list of what you want and then you simply let the numbers game do the work.'

'Playing the numbers game with a prepared list gets results. The damsel in distress and the guy on a white horse only exist in fairytales.'

Graham Steele

While Graham Steele's approach could be considered extreme by some people, he demonstrates that when you have a clearly written list of what you want in a partner and you state upfront what you have to offer, the numbers game will work just as well in love as it does in business.

Who You Should Avoid

The person you don't want is someone who is desperate or under pressure to find a partner. This was the case for past generations of humans and it worked well for them because their life expectancy was much shorter than ours, they had 6–12 children and were concerned with basic survival, not with satisfying each other's emotional needs. There are people out there today who want you as their partner because of their own external pressures, such as to please their family, 'It's that stage of life', 'All my friends are doing it', 'It's probably time for me to settle down', 'I won't get anyone better', 'If I don't marry them, they'll leave me', 'This could be the change in life I'm looking for', 'I need to have a baby before it's too late' and so on. You've heard them all before.

You also don't want the clingy, needy type who can be recognised by the 20 phone messages they leave asking where you are, the barrage of emails and gifts they send, or who tell you they can't live without you or they're in a bad relationship and want an escape route. In other words, you should avoid anyone who intends to make *you* responsible for their happiness. It's hard enough being responsible for your own happiness without taking on someone else's problems.

They'll make all the promises necessary to convince you that being with them is in your best interest. They're like the person who buys the Super Duper Ab-Master they saw on late-night TV – deep down they know that it's a waste of time and money and that it will soon be shoved under the bed.

Remember that all relationships aren't for ever – most will be simply fun and a stepping stone to bigger and better things. Approach relationships on this basis and don't look for perfection in every relationship. Look at each date you have as a fun, short-term relationship that may or may not work out in the long term.

Clues About Mr/Ms Wrong

Overall, men love women's bodies in all shapes and sizes, while women don't have men's body shapes as a high priority in a potential partner. Anyone who wants you to look like the people on the cover of *Glamour Magazine* or *Men's Health* won't want you in the long term for who you are. These are usually insecure people who need a handbag on their arm in public to bolster their own insecurities or their lack of self-esteem. It's all about them, not you. Only a small percentage of people can rate ten out of ten in the Mating Rating stakes, and they are attracted to others with the same rating. Most of us are less than perfect and so our ideal mate also has imperfections.

That's why we are attracted to and form long-term relationships with those who have the same Mating Rating as us. If a person has a Mating Rating of, say, seven out of ten, they will be attracted to someone who is also a seven. They may admire or lust after someone who rates a ten, but most will eventually settle for someone with the same score as themselves. The fact that they have flaws like us makes them more real and more human. After the attachment stage, they will love you even more because of your shortcomings. That's how long-term love works. This is why the person who constantly finds faults in you and is always nit-picking has not entered the attachment stage and is *not* the person for you.

When the Chemistry Is Wrong

Bella joined a new tennis club and the people she met were fun to be around. One of the big attractions at the club was a cute guy called Sam. He was the life of the party and Bella had spent a lot of time getting to know him. She found him very down to earth and discovered that they had a lot in common. They had the same philosophical and spiritual beliefs, they both enjoyed an energetic lifestyle, their communication was excellent, they were both successful in their careers, were good with money, and both wanted to have kids by the age of 30. Plus, he was great to look at and Bella loved his smile.

She knew that Sam was attracted to her as much as she was to him but he never asked her out on a date – it was always with other people around. She decided that on Valentine's Day she would ask him out. She asked and he enthusiastically agreed. She booked the restaurant, bought a new outfit and was excited about finally taking the relationship to the next level.

Valentine's Day was wonderful and the meal was very romantic. The restaurant was closing at midnight but neither wanted the night to end. Sam suggested a coffee at his place – Bella agreed. As they sat on the sofa in his apartment, he took

her in his arms and kissed her passionately. But Bella felt
nothing. No chemistry whatsoever. Zero reaction. It was like
kissing a squid. Bella decided it was time to go. Driving
home, she realised Sam was everything that she wanted in a
man but there was just no chemistry between them. Nothing.
She felt sad because she believed that Sam could be the one
for her, but he just didn't do it for her. They remained friends
but never dated again.

If the chemistry isn't there with someone, your relationship will always be a logical, orderly one. The ability to create a chemical reaction in a partner is what sustains long-term passion and desire. There are two types of chemical reaction: natural and created. Natural passion happens when hardwired factors come into play, such as immune-system difference, pheromones and our love-map criteria. Sustained passion is when both partners continually work at creating an environment for passion to flourish.

The 9% Rule

Evolutionary psychologists Peter Todd at Indiana University and Geoffrey Miller (author of *The Mating Mind*) at the University of New Mexico used a computer simulation to determine mathematically how someone chooses from a number of possible partners at a party that has, say, 100 potential partners. They found that by the time we have assessed 9 possibilities of the 100 in the room, we have decided what our aspirations will be. This means that at the party with 100 possible mates, you only have to study the first 9 you randomly encounter before you choose. Examining less than 9% means you won't have enough information to make a good choice; examining more makes it likely you'll pass up a good choice. This fascinating experiment gives you a clear message – if you only have limited time, don't search indefinitely before picking a mate, because you'll either run out of time or possible partners. After you've checked out 9% of the available talent, you're ready.

Summary

It takes at least a year and a few good arguments to begin to know who someone really is. Finding a suitable mate is a logical process that needs to be approached in the same way you would approach hiring someone to run your business. Never commit yourself to any person in the early stages of a relationship because you are crazy in love – it's likely to just be your hormones talking. Hormones eventually subside, and when they do, you'll be left looking at the cold, hard facts about whether or not this person is suitable to live your life with. Doesn't it make more sense to undertake this evaluation *before* a new relationship gets too far down the track?

It's your life and you are responsible for it. A great myth is 'When you're not looking, that's when you'll find true love.' This old cliché will definitely prevent you from taking positive action with your love life, so forget it. Write a list of the minimum you'll accept in a partner and stick to it. Don't commit early to anyone, and never settle for second best in your relationships – and don't let anyone put you second. If you feel that a person has what you want to make your life easy and fun, encourage that relationship. If they don't but it still feels good, stay with it till it wears off, then move on. Never use someone as an interim measure until 'the right person comes along' – that causes more pain than pleasure, prevents you from focusing on what you really want and is an abuse of the other person.

Write a detailed list of exactly what things you want in an ideal partner and then become socially active so you meet as many people as you possibly can. Play the numbers game. Why settle for second best when there are about 1.52 million potential perfect partners in the world for you right now? But you've got to be active and get out among them. Don't wait to be discovered.

You will need to kiss a lot of frogs to find your prince or princess. You need to be committed to obtain your dream and it takes a lot of hard work to make it happen. Start right now – write your list.

Many people believe that there is one perfect partner out there, somewhere, waiting for them. The reality is that there are over 1.52 million perfect matches out there for each of us.

- Work out your Mating Rating and look for partners with the same Mating Rating as you.
- Commit yourself to finding the right person – write a list and stick to it.
- If the chemistry isn't right, move on.
- Don't give up! There are plenty of people out there who are perfect for you.

Chapter 8
15 Mysteries About Men Women Don't Understand

The information in the next two chapters is about men and women and their urges, desires and obsessions. If you are a female reader, some things about men may surprise you, shock you or even make you angry. It's important to understand that we will be talking directly and plainly about these things and have not sugar-coated them to be politically correct or to say what someone might like to hear. When you have a realistic understanding of these things, the opposite sex becomes easier to handle and to live with.

There are many things that irritate, annoy and infuriate men about women, but top of the list is sex. Men want sex any time, often all the time. There are plenty of statistics around demonstrating that a 40-year-old man thinks about sex once every 4 minutes and an 18-year-old once every 11 seconds. The

Kinsey Institute at Indiana University says that 54% of men think about sex at least every day, 43% think about it a few times a week or month, and 4% once a month or less. Women, on the other hand, are popularly believed to think about sex rarely – and then only when there's absolutely nothing else on the agenda.

Sex is often the basis of the tension that arises between men and women, both within relationships and outside. All research shows that sex is the single biggest factor in couples having problems getting on with each other, whether it's about different levels of desire, different timing of desire or simply one person no longer fancying the other. When it comes to complaints about sex, men usually say there is not enough, while women claim there is too much. The question is, does lack of sex contribute to a bad relationship, or does a bad relationship lead to less sex? The answer is both.

It's reasonable to assume that man's erotic instincts remain constant in every generation, and denying this fact means that the expressions of those instincts causes pressure in relationships. Squeezing a balloon does not eliminate the air; it merely forces the same air to distort the balloon's skin in another area.

1. Why Men Wake Up In the Morning With an Erection

Any woman who has ever had a love relationship with a man knows that she doesn't need an alarm clock to wake her in the morning – instead, as the sun rises, so does his penis and she feels it poking her in the back. This is caused by two things. Firstly, a man's testosterone level is highest at sunrise, just before he sets out for the day's hunt, and it is lowest at sunset. Nature ensures he has a last opportunity to pass on his genes before he heads off – in case he doesn't return. Second, the erectile nerves that instruct the penis to stand to attention are wrapped round the prostate gland, which sits immediately below the bladder. A full bladder presses on the erectile nerves and can make the penis rise. Because a man is not psychologically or visually aroused at sunrise, however, the best a woman can usually expect is a morning quickie as Mother Nature completes her sunrise task.

> **Bob woke up at 6 a.m. to find his wife jabbing him in the back with a broom handle. 'What's going on?' he demanded. She replied, 'You try it for a change!'**

2. Why Sex Can Be Just Sex for Men

Professors Raquel and Ruben Gur at the University of Pennsylvania School of Medicine are the MRI pioneers who found that the anterior commissure, which connects the left and right brain hemispheres, is 12% smaller in men than in women and that the corpus callosum – the cord that lets one brain hemisphere exchange information with the other – has up to 30% less connections in men than in women. These differences account for why men are better at working in one mode at a time. Imagine that most male brains are a honeycomb of small rooms, each containing one specific skill that operates independently of others. This gives men their 'one-thing-at-a-time' approach to everything they do and is why they can focus more intensely on single tasks than women. Having a 'mono-tracking' brain lets men focus intently on either sex *or* love. Sex can be just sex, and love can be just love – and occasionally they happen together. This allows men to do something that women don't understand: have sex with women they don't like.

> **It's great to be a man because it doesn't preclude you from having great sex with women you don't even like.**

For a man, it can be just sex and then he can forget about it. He doesn't need to discuss it or ever bring it up again, unless he's bragging to his friends. When a cheating man is asked by a woman why he had sex with another woman and he claims, 'It was just sex,' he's probably telling the truth. Men's brains can compartmentalise sex into a simple activity like shaving – after you've had a shave, you don't think about it again till next time. But to a woman, 'It was just sex' is not a believable response. For her, love and sex switch on together in the brain, and one is the consequence of the other. In fact, one usually equals the other. Sex is rarely just about sex for a woman – there must be some feeling attached to it. If not, she's likely to be using it to boost her self-esteem. Even if a woman has the urge to have sex just for physical gratification, she still searches for a man who appears to fit at least part of her list of appropriate partners. Not so for a man – when he feels the urge, all he needs is something with a hole in it. For men, sex and love don't necessarily happen together.

> **Men can't make love and answer questions at the same time. So, no talking, please, ladies.**

On a deep level, most women seem to understand this, yet they will still get upset when the 'sex-is-sex' aspect of male behaviour shows itself in such ways as ogling other women, reading lingerie catalogues, looking at porn and complaining that he 'just wants me for sex' or has 'kinky' requests.

3. The Nothing Room

As we have said, the male brain is like a honeycomb of rooms and each room has its own special function. One room may contain spatial ability, the next has speech function, another has love and so on. But most men have a special room that many women don't have and don't understand – it's called the 'Nothing Room'. Its name describes exactly what happens in this room – nothing. Not only is it empty, it's a favourite room for most men. This is a place where a man's mind goes when he's fishing, watching TV or just sitting in a chair with a blank look on his face. The 'Nothing Room' has a purpose – to regenerate mental energy. A man needs four to five short meditations each day when he visits the Nothing Room to re-energise. Women do not have this same brain need, so when a man is in it, they will ask, 'What are you thinking?' When he answers, 'Nothing,' the woman sees this as a lie and accuses him of concealing things from her. He thought he was just going to chill out for ten minutes and suddenly he's in an argument about thinking nothing. When a man says he's thinking about nothing, it's usually true. He's also deaf at the time, so don't discuss anything important with him – write him a note.

4. Why Men Are Obsessed With Women's Breasts

Women everywhere are dumbfounded by the obsession that men have with breasts. Breast augmentation is now one of the most widely performed operations in the world and shows the lengths women will go to get their share of men's attention.

Only female humans have buttocks and breasts. Other female primates have mammary glands inside the chest and long nipples for feeding. Most of female human breast tissue is fat, which serves no apparent purpose – or does it? Like most mammals, human males once only mounted their females from behind and the female fleshy buttocks served as a signalling system. Now that humans stand on two legs and face each other, the female buttock display has evolved on the chest to mimic the round buttock lobes that attract males. They might not know it, but that's why women wear push-up bras and boob-tubes, and have surgery to enhance their cleavage. In *The Definitive Book of Body Language* we revealed how we had conducted photographic tests in which men were asked to differentiate between a butt crack and a boob crack – no men could tell the difference but they all found both cracks very stimulating.

So, ladies, should you encourage men to breast-gaze? No, it's not necessary. He doesn't need encouragement. He'll do it anyway.

5. Why Men Won't Tell the Truth to Women About Sex

To avoid conflict, most men tell women what they want to hear. As males become older and more experienced, they become more and more comfortable at telling lies to women about love and sex. It's not because men want to lie, it's because women are often unhappy about hearing the truth when they ask a question. Although most men will deny it, lying to women is something they become good at and it's a game women encourage men to play. From a man's standpoint, a white lie, a half-truth or some believable line, such as how his partner is the only woman he ever wants to have sex with, is usually a safe option and avoids being sent to sleep on the sofa. When another woman wiggles past with her boobs hanging out, however, a man's brain is wired to take it all in and he receives a shot of dopamine for a feel-good response. His body is specifically designed for this reaction and it has little to do with his feelings or love for his partner. When his partner accuses him of ogling, his usual first reaction is to lie, lie and deny. 'Darling, I wasn't looking', 'You're much more attractive than her', 'Why would I look at her when I've got you?' and so on – you've heard the lines. When a woman takes this accusatory path with a man, she trains him to lie to avoid negative consequences for himself and to protect her feelings.

> **'I wasn't looking at her breasts, darling –
> they were obscuring my view!'**

Interestingly, the studies we discussed in *Why Men Lie &*
Women Cry about lying and deception show that three out of
four women admitted to lying to men to gain an advantage.
While 73% of women say they flirted with a man or used hints
of the possibility of sex to gain a favour or benefit, only half
the men reported that they were aware of lies being 'planted'
on them. In contrast, 71% of men admit to lying to a woman
to get her to have sex with him for example, exaggerating how
significant a woman was in their life or saying, 'I love,' when
they didn't mean it – but 97% of women report that they were
aware of such lies being told.

If a woman teaches a man to lie about little things, however, he'll soon become confident in lying about bigger things.
And whether women will admit it or not, they feel more secure
when men lie to them about sex. Men learn early that talking
in terms of a woman's value keeps her around longer and
keeps her off his case.

The ten biggest lies men tell women about sex and love

The following lies are used by men everywhere and are told to
women when the consequences of telling the truth are too
severe. Of the women we asked to comment on these lies, 75%

said their male partner would never use them, yet 85% of men admit to having told some of them at some time in their past relationships.

1 **'I'd never cheat on you.'** If Beyoncé threw herself naked at his feet, he would definitely consider his options. It doesn't mean he would do it, it means he'd definitely consider it, and research shows around half *would* do it. Denial is a safe option because such opportunities rarely ever present themselves anyway.

2 **'I would never/have never been to a strip club.'** Given the controls put on men by women and society, they definitely won't admit to this one. And yes, men definitely would like to have sex with those strippers.

3 **'I'm not into that sort of thing.'** Men use this lie in response to a woman's repulsion to a kinky sex act she's seen on TV or to her interrogation into what he wants from sex. The reality is, he'd love to try it.

4 **'I've never thought about sleeping with your friends.'** No, especially not the one with the sporty body and the big boobs. He's always thinking about it, even about the ugly ones. It doesn't mean he'll do it, it means he thinks about it whether you like it or not.

5 **'I'm not interested in porn.'** Yeah, right. So he's the only man in the world who has never accessed the multi-trillion-dollar Internet porn business. An estimated 68% of Internet sites visited are porn, but he's never seen one? It's easier to believe in Santa Claus than this.

6 **'I've never imagined that chick on the reception desk giving me a blowjob.'** Well, not since he saw her last anyway. The fact that you call her a 'cheap tart' makes her even more attractive because she's more likely to have sex with him.

7 **'I'm happy to give up my life for you.'** No, he's not, but with the trade-off of regular sex, some mothering, cooked meals, a clean house and less aggravation in his life, he'll do it till further notice.

8 **'I don't think about sex with every woman I meet.'** Not only does he mentally undress every woman he sees, he imagines the repertoire of positions he could try with them, and sometimes he thinks about them when he has sex with you. He will definitely deny this one.

9 **'I'd never lie to you.'** He will tell you whatever is necessary to avoid tears or conflict with you. If you challenge the lie, he'll say it was necessary because you can't handle the truth.

10 **'I wasn't looking at her boobs.'** He definitely *was* looking at them but he lies because he doesn't want trouble from you. Women can't handle the truth, remember?

Men would prefer to tell women the complete truth about sex but men don't want to deal with the consequences of doing so.

Any woman who reads out the above lies to a man will usually be greeted with a response like 'No! That's not true of me! The authors have got it wrong!' No...we've done our research, and one of us (the authors) is a man. Most men will acknowledge the truth about these lies or tell jokes to each other about them, but they would never tell any woman who may provide them with benefits that they do this.

In summary, most men will do and say whatever is necessary to keep women happy, to get them off their backs and get more sex. They will serve up as much charm, sincerity, compliments, attention, kindness and romantic acts as it takes to get a woman's attention and keep her placated. This male characteristic can be seen by women as insincere, conspiring and manipulative, but men see it as a form of self-defence. It's not good or bad – it's just the way it is, so accept it and manage men within the confines of these behaviours. The bottom line is that a relationship is always based on an exchange of goods and services.

6. Why Men Love Curvy Women

The 'hourglass' figure has been the focus of art for thousands of years and it is the woman's curves, not her weight or fat content that matters.

At puberty, a rise in oestrogen causes fat deposits to accumulate on the hips and upper thighs of girls, to be used as a source of food in the event of hard times and for breastfeeding. In a series of 12 tests, psychologist Devendra Singh discovered that a hips-to-waist ratio of 0.67 to 0.8 is an accurate indicator of a woman's reproductive status and is, subsequently, the ratio most attractive to men. This ratio means that a woman's waist measurement is 70% of the measurement of her hips. In these studies, Singh tested how attracted men were to female figures and found that the 0.7 hips-to-waist ratio was without doubt the most attractive, regardless of the amount of body fat a woman had. In other words, even if the woman was overweight, she was still seen as attractive if she had the right ratio.

Singh analysed 30 years of *Playboy* centrefolds and found that, even though the centrefold women became thinner over the years, the 70% hips-to-waist ratio was a constant. Ratios higher than 70% revealed lower levels of health and fertility, as did ratios lower than 70%. The wrong ratio meant that a woman had significantly less chance of becoming pregnant and successfully carrying a man's genes.

We analysed the paintings of the Old Masters and found that, even though the women painted then were much larger than today's models, the 70% hips-to-waist ratio remained a constant.

In the British Safeway poll of 500 people, 87% of men said they liked a woman to be curvaceous and the right weight for her height, and the vast majority of men preferred a woman to be curvy rather than thin. Only 8% preferred 'very thin, bordering on underweight' women, while 92% liked 'voluptuous' women. Interestingly, the response was almost identical among women, with 88% thinking curvaceous women were a bigger turn-on for men than thin women. So when it comes to an attractive female body, as far as men are concerned it's about shape, not weight.

7. Why the G-Spot Is Like a UFO

A UFO is a mythical object that most men have heard of but no one seems to be able to find. The G-spot is a group of nerve endings covering up to 3 square centimeters usually located on the front upper area of the vagina. It's the place where the nerve endings of the clitoris intersect, and while it's strong in some women, it can be weak or non-responsive in others. It was 'discovered' by Dr Ernst Grafenberg in 1950 he never mentioned how he discovered it. Because of its front-upper location, doggy-style sex is usually the best way for the penis to stimulate it.

> **The most common sex position for married couples is doggy style. The husband sits up and begs. The wife rolls over and plays dead.**

Because most men have little idea what the G-spot is all about, it becomes incumbent on a woman to teach him where it is and to tell him what to do with it.

8. Why It's So Important to Men for Women to Initiate Sex

Making an approach to a woman carries huge risks, and most men have fragile egos because rejection is seen as a failure on their part. If a woman refuses, a man can feel crushed. In the animal kingdom, the majority of male creatures simply have to show their sex organs to the female of their species to initiate sex. For animals, it's rare for the female to laugh, turn away or say she has a headache. Men have to deal with this kind of rejection regularly, however, and it doesn't get any easier with experience. This is why most men would love the woman in their life to make the first move far more often. It eases their feeling of obligation to initiate sex and makes them feel desired and important. Men can often achieve this by being much more attentive and loving to the woman in their life, which will usually make her feel more inclined to suggest sex. If men practised subtlety, they would end up getting what they wanted more often than if they simply asked.

> **A man is like a fine wine. He starts out as raw as grapes, and it's a woman's job to stomp on him and keep him in the dark until he matures into something she'd like to have dinner with.**

Most women wish their men would take the hint, but few women will tell them directly. Women seem to believe that somehow men will pick up their subtle clues, but it only leaves men confused.

9. Why Men Get It So Wrong In Nightclubs

Women who dance provocatively in a nightclub do so to let men know that they might be available to the right person. Men, however, read it as saying they might be available to anyone or everyone. This creates a major area of conflict because of the different ways men and women perceive a woman's availability. The problem is that men act on their assumptions and are likely to decode friendliness as sexual availability.

Early studies in 1982 by Dr Antonia Abbey, Department of Community Medicine, Wayne State University, Detroit and later studies by psychologists Saal, Johnson and Weber of Kansas State University, confirm this. Using actors, they conducted an experiment in which a junior female visited the office of a senior male to discuss a business deadline. The actors were told to be friendly and not flirtatious in any way. Respondents were then asked to watch the video and assess the intentions of the actors. Women watching the interaction said that the female actor was only trying to be friendly (92%) and not sexy or seductive (27%). Men also perceived her as being friendly (87%), but at the same time saw her as being sexy or seductive (55%). In other words, men are twice as likely as women to infer sexual intentions that don't exist and to act on that assumption. In evolutionary terms, this evolved strategy makes sense because even if a man only got it right a fraction of the time, it still gave him an increased chance of keeping his genes moving forward. Another study showed that if a man discovers a woman is carrying a condom in her purse, his assumption of her sexual intentions multiplies by four. Most women are aware of this 'over-assumption' and can exploit it by playing up to a man for benefits. This is commonly known as 'cock-teasing'.

10. When Is a Man Ready for Commitment or Marriage?

In simple biological terms, the 21st-century man will become Mr Right when his testosterone begins to decline. That's around age 27. Past generations of men were married in their teens, as sex was one of the benefits of marriage. For today's young (and older) men, getting plenty of sex is no longer an issue. It's available anywhere, anytime and from a range of different women. Consequently, many of today's younger men think, Why get stuck in eternal monogamy when I can spread my seed far and wide?

From around age 27, a man starts to become more caring

and passive because his ratio of female to male hormones begins to change direction. He becomes more interested in long-term relationships and begins to think more with his big head than his little one. He will phone a woman for no partic- ular reason and will even cancel a sports date with his mates to go somewhere with her. In the lust and romantic love stages of a relationship, men are high on male hormones and are usu- ally impetuous or over-enthusiastic towards a woman in their initial contact – big bunches of flowers are delivered to her at her workplace so that everyone knows about it, he books romantic dinners at expensive restaurants and uses well-worn expressions of his love. After sex, however, he's the guy who feels the urge to get out of bed as soon as possible and do something, anything – watch TV, call someone, fix his car, send emails, cook or, if he can't do any of those things, fall asleep. Anything but be emotionally in bed with the woman. His brain goes into its default mode, which shouts, 'The jobs done here – now, what's next?' This usually happens after five sex sessions with the same woman because his brain under- stands that, statistically speaking, five times is enough sex with one female for her to conceive. This is why – unless he's considering her as a longer-term partner – he starts to lose interest in her by session number six, regardless of how acro- batic she may be. If he meets a new female he likes, however, he'll immediately be raring to go again.

After five sexual encounters, Mr Wrong loses interest in a woman, just as it is with the males of other animal species.

This 'five-sex-sessions' phenomenon is also seen in other species, such as male sheep, cows and pigs. After they have mated an average of five times with one female, the males have trouble getting it up again for an encore. Even when the same

> **When a woman marries, she expects the three 'S's: sensitivity, sincerity and sharing. What does she get? The three 'B's: burps, body odour and beer breath.**

females are disguised with rugs, perfume and have bags over their heads, the males still can't perform. Introduce a new female, however, and the male's penis will stand to attention. Mother Nature knows what she's doing – she says, 'You've done the best you can do after five times. Now go and find another female and help perpetuate your species.' That's why Mr Wrong loses interest early, stops making an effort and it becomes obvious that it's all about him once again.

Men seeking long-term relationships often start out the same way as men seeking a one-night stand, but when they experience the feelings of long-term attachment, they begin to stay in bed longer and talk, touch or exhibit other typical female behaviours.

11. Why Mature Men Wear Speedos in Public or Proudly Display a Pot Belly

Men's lack of awareness about how they look in public has always been a mystery to women. Most women are experts at sucking in their stomach in public or avoiding sitting at an angle of 90 degrees in a bikini in case a small roll of fat can be seen. It's commonplace, however, to see a man who looks nine months pregnant sending smiles and gazes to a woman across a room, or a man wearing Speedo budgie-smugglers having a conversation with several women, apparently oblivious to the fact that his Speedos were never taught that it's impolite to point.

Men are silently aware that their value on the mating market is largely dependent on their ability to gather resources, not how they look. For a woman, any success she may have

Most men have better a
body image than women.

with resources can be seen as a threat to men, whereas her physical appearance and potential to produce offspring are regarded as a premium. While she needs to wear a black skirt to keep her butt looking small, he only needs a Rolex or a BMW to counter a fat gut.

12. Men and Their Fetishes

A fetish is an external stimulus that makes a connection between a past mental experience and sexual feelings. Much of this behaviour comes from childhood and adolescence. The fetish triggers the sex drive and makes the person want to relive the fetish scenario. It may be a related piece of clothing, a smell, a colour, a fabric, obesity or old age. You name it – whether it's a shoe or a salmon, an ankle or a toothbrush – some guy somewhere has a fetish for it. When men fantasise, they imagine body parts, shapes and positions – they don't visualise whether a woman is a great homemaker, whether she can sing or if she wants world peace. The porn sites on the Internet are flooded with fetish images of every type imaginable, and 99% of the viewers of these sites are believed to be male.

> **Once upon a time, a man asked a woman
> to marry him.
> She said, 'No!' and so he lived happily ever after,
> played golf a lot, drank beer, went fishing
> and farted whenever he wanted.**

Because men are so stimulated by visual images, over 90% of what is classified as 'deviant' behaviour involves men. Around 97% of all convictions in the US involving peering through someone's window are against men. For the same motivations, men visit strip clubs and look at girly magazines.

13. What Men Worry About

Like women, men worry about their flaws, but they don't let them control their lives as women do. Here's what men worry about most:

> Is my gut too big?
> Do I look too young/old?
> Do I look masculine enough?
> Am I losing my hair?
> Will I be successful?
> Can I satisfy a woman sexually?
> Is my penis too small?
> Will I be able to provide for my family?
> Will I ever have enough money?
> Will any woman love me the way I am?

Men think and worry about these things but will rarely mention them to anyone. And you'll *never* hear a man say to his male friends, 'Hey, guys, do you think I'm an unsuccessful, balding, fat slob who's a lousy dresser with a little dick?' Men don't like mentioning their failings to anyone. You shouldn't mention them either, as it can be crushing to a man's ego and create tension in the relationship.

14. Why Men Have Difficulty Saying, 'I Love You'

For most people, 'I love you' is blurted out near the beginning of a relationship, when both partners are high on hormones and probably have trouble remembering even their own names. For a woman, she's likely to start exhibiting nesting behaviours, such as picking curtains, cuddling teddy bears, cooking meals for him (if she doesn't already), noticing couples with babies everywhere and talking in 'happily-ever-after' terms. Typically, this time becomes scary for a man, and he may even wish he'd never said, 'I love you.' He must live up to this statement and its implications today, tomorrow or maybe for ever. So unless he's hoping to have sex with a woman and is in a rush of hormones, he'll avoid saying it.

Life Rules for Men No. 39
Never join your girlfriend or wife in criticising one of your male friends, except if she's withholding sex pending your response.

A woman stays in a relationship with an unsuitable man under the illusion that he'll change now he's with her or that 'Love conquers all.' She refuses to acknowledge that he treats her badly or doesn't really love her. She doesn't even notice how she's slipped from his 'beautiful princess' to 'bitch' in just six months. If a woman is unsure of a man's love, she can ask her closest female friends for their opinion and insist they tell the truth. In other words, phone a friend or ask the audience. While many women are not good at spotting deficiencies in their own relationships, they are excellent at spotting them in other couples. Most women don't realise how little love existed in a relationship until they are out of it, but a woman's female friends can 'see' the truth, so ask them.

Men love to meet women who profess that 'Love conquers all' – it means that with a good delivery of the right 'love phrases' at the right time, she'll be easy to get into bed.

15. The Top Five Questions That Frighten Most Men

1. 'What are you thinking about?'
2. 'Do you love me?'
3. 'Do I look fat?'
4. 'Do you think she is prettier than me?'
5. 'What would you do if I died?'

What makes these questions so difficult for a man to deal with is that they are all guaranteed to explode into a major argument if he answers incorrectly – that is, if he tells the truth. Below is an analysis of each question, along with possible responses.

Question 1: 'What are you thinking about?'

The proper answer to this is, 'I'm sorry if I have been a bit distant, darling. I was just reflecting on what a warm, wonderful, thoughtful, caring, intelligent woman you are, and how lucky I am to have you in my life.' This response obviously bears no resemblance to the truth, which most likely is one of the following:

a. 'Nothing.'
b. 'Football.'
c. 'Angelina Jolie, naked.'
d. 'How fat you are.'
e. 'How I would spend the insurance money if you died.'

Question 2: 'Do you love me?'

The correct response is, 'Yes! I'm crazy about you!'
Inappropriate responses include:
 a. 'Sure! Heaps! Can we have sex now?'
 b. 'Would it make you feel better if I said yes?'
 c. 'Can you define the word "love"?'
 d. 'I'm your husband…That's my job.'
 e. 'I have sex with you, don't I?'
 f. 'Who, me?'

Question 3: 'Do I look fat?'

The correct answer is an emphatic 'Absolutely not! You look
perfect!' Among the incorrect answers are:

 a. 'Compared to what?'
 b. 'I wouldn't call you fat, but you're not exactly thin.'
 c. 'A little extra weight looks good on you.'
 d. 'I've seen fatter.'
 e. 'No. I inadvertently put a twenty-kilo weight on the scales
  when you were on them.'
 f. 'Could you repeat the question? I was just thinking about
  how I would spend the insurance money if you died.'

Question 4: 'Do you think she is prettier than me?'

Once again, the proper response is an emphatic 'Definitely
not!' Incorrect responses include:

 a. 'Yes, but you have a better personality.'
 b. 'Not prettier, but definitely thinner.'
 c. 'Not as pretty as you when you were her age.'
 d. 'Define "pretty".'
 e. 'Could you repeat the question? I was just thinking about
  how I would spend the insurance money if you died.'

Question 5: 'What would you do if I died?'

This is a definite no-win question, whatever a man says. The real answer is, 'Buy a Ferrari and a boat', but here's a typical way this question could be handled:

WOMAN: Would you get married again?
MAN: Definitely not!
WOMAN: Why not? Don't you like being married?
MAN: Yes! I love being married!
WOMAN: Then why wouldn't you remarry?
MAN: OK, then…I'd get married again.
WOMAN: (*with a hurt look on her face*) You would?
MAN: Well…uh…you asked me!
WOMAN: Would you sleep with her in our bed?
MAN: Where else would we sleep?
WOMAN: Would you replace my photos with pictures of her?
MAN: Well…that would seem the appropriate thing to do.
WOMAN: And would you let her use my golf clubs?
MAN: She can't. She's left-handed.

- A man's brain has the ability to separate love from sex. Occasionally they happen together.
- Men lie to women to avoid conflict. Never ask a man a question if you don't want to hear the truth, otherwise you are simply training him to lie.
- If you want to make the man in your life happy, initiate sex more often.
- Men are just as insecure about their flaws as women are; they just don't like to discuss them. Never point out a man's failings – you'll only create tension and bruise his ego.

Chapter 9
12 Truths About Women Most Men Don't Know

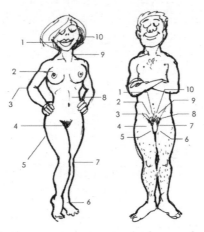

The key erotic zones on the human body.

Today, arguments about sex are much more intense than they were in past generations. Men see few reasons for women to be reserved about sex. If women are on the Pill or use another form of birth control, why don't they want sex more often? After women's liberation, men felt women would be more ready to initiate sex. Women declared they were willing to ignore society's past expectations about women not wanting much sex and men assumed, happily, that suddenly they'd be regularly asked by for sex and that women would no longer be coy about men's advances. Women began buying porn, sex toys and talking about men as sex objects. They insisted on being free to dress as seductively as they wanted, wherever they wanted. Women's magazines continually had articles about how to please men in bed. Radio programmes for women featured sex counsellors talking about technique, and there were explicit television shows about sex. Men were excited and enthusiastic. Women, it was proclaimed, would now want sex as much as men.

This, however, was an anticlimax (no pun intended). The sexual revolution arrived, but after all the loud talk about free sex, many women soon settled back into their default position – being passive sexual partners. Some didn't, but most did. Once again, men found themselves being cast as always wanting sex while trying to deal with women who rarely did. Many men had expected life to be like living with the girls from the Playboy Mansion, but they were in fact back to living with Mother Teresa. Contrary to what many men believe, women do want sex and they often want it more often than they'll actually say.

If the state of a woman's relationship is bad, it will cause her to avoid sex. A man in the same relationship is perfectly happy to have sex anytime because, as we saw in the last chapter, his brain has the ability to separate love from sex, and sex usually carries a higher priority for him because of the need to continue the species. They can have sex at virtually anytime, anyplace and under almost any circumstances. For women, it's the complete opposite. Many women can't understand how a man can have sex without feeling emotion at the same time, and most resent this. Women's different sex centre in the brain and significantly lower level of testosterone means the need for sex is further down their priority list.

Below are 12 key areas about women and sex that most men don't understand.

1. What Women Want From Sex

The present-day obsession with being politically correct has created the illusion that women want the same things from sex as men. Many magazines and television shows suggest that not only do women have the same criteria as men for good sex, they also have the same sex drive. The Women's Rights Movement has pushed for and obtained equality in many areas, and society has erroneously concluded that the same applies to sex. Nothing could be further from the truth.

> **The fortune-teller told a young man, 'To live a happy life, you need to find a girl with similar interests to you and who wants to do the same things as you.'**
> **'What? Getting drunk and picking up women?'**
> **he gasped. 'I'll need an alcoholic lesbian!'**

Over a 30-year period, we collected and analysed hundreds of studies and surveys about what women want from sex. These included studies carried out by universities and health institutes, professional sex researchers such as Kinsey and popular magazines such as *Cosmopolitan* and *Redbook*. We have drawn two important conclusions from all this. First, a woman's motivations to have sex are no different now than they have been for thousands of years. Almost every study shows that the high-powered businesswoman, the woman at home with children and the woman who crouched in a cave 100,000 years ago have the same criteria for rating good sex. Second, a 21st-century woman's sex drive is no stronger today than that of her ancestors – all that has changed is that sex is now open for discussion and is on display in the media. At the top of her list is finding the right partner who either has resources or has the ability to get them.

Here's a summary of the top five things most women say they want from men before they will feel like sex:

1. To feel attractive and special.
2. To feel loved and protected.

3. To be pampered and spoiled.
4. To be kissed, touched and cuddled.
5. To talk about her feelings.

Compare this list to the top five of what most men say they want from women:

1. For her to say 'Yes' to sex more often.
2. To have more spontaneous sex.
3. For her to initiate sex more often and be creative.
4. Not to make him feel guilty about his sexual needs.
5. To understand he is mainly motivated by visual signals, such as lingerie.

A woman wants the lead-up to sex to go slowly. In fact, she doesn't even use the word 'sex'– she wants to 'make love' or to 'sleep' with someone. After sex, she wants to continue to talk about her feelings, but many women complain that this is not possible – because he's asleep.

> **A man's number-one fantasy is being in bed with two women.**
> **Women also want this so they'll have someone to talk to when their partner falls asleep.**

These lists show how women want lots of emotional input first, while men want a wild, uninhibited romp. Because of our different basic drives and priorities, it's not unreasonable to say that men and women are incompatible when it comes to sex. Women frequently describe men as 'selfish' and 'always in a hurry', and men describe women as 'unimaginative' and 'mechanical'. A woman may even describe a man's need for erotic images as 'disgusting' or 'sick'. He describes her need to go slow as 'uncreative' and 'boring'. When you understand and accept that male and female brains are wired differently, that each has a different perspective of sex and love, that each has different priorities, you can make the necessary changes to your approach to sex and you will soon be described as an outstanding lover. The ideal sex life is one in which each partner withholds judgement of the other's needs and, instead, fulfils those needs. Our sexual needs are different – not better or worse, different.

> **While the airforce plane was idling on the runway, one of the female crew gave the soldiers on board the safety information regarding seat belts and emergency exits.**
> **Finally, she said, 'Now sit back and enjoy your trip while your captain, Joanne Parish, and her crew fly you safely to Iraq.'**
> **An old sergeant sitting in the front row asked, 'Did I hear you right? Is the captain a woman?'**
> **'Yes!' said the attendant, 'In fact, this entire crew is female.'**
> **'My God,' he said nervously, 'I don't know what to think with only women up there in the cockpit!'**
> **'Oh, that's another thing, Sergeant,' she said. 'It's no longer called the cockpit...it's the Box Office.'**

2. Why Women So Rarely Initiate Sex

This is the number-one complaint men have about women in nearly every country. The reason is simple: as we have repeatedly pointed out, men are built to have a far stronger sex drive than women, men having between 10 and 20 times more testosterone and a larger hypothalamus, the brain area where hormones stimulate the desire for sex.

'My wife says she loves me, but she never seems to want to show me. She seems to think it's enough to say nice things to

me and do little things for me, like making my favourite meal
or doing the laundry, but I don't really care about any of that.
I can do those things myself. What I'd love her to do one day
is dress up for me in a sexy little outfit and greet me like that
when I come home from work. That would really show me
that she loves me. But I've got as much chance of that as
going to the moon. I mean, if she really cared, wouldn't she
want to make me happy?'   Ian

Over the past million years, men evolved to be sex-driven to
continue our species. Women evolved to be the carriers of children. Women's primary drive was to be carers and protectors
so that they could nurture the children and keep them safe.
Nothing has changed. Women also extend this to the men in
their lives, and like to comfort, support and keep them safe.
Men, however, see every cuddle as foreplay. Their focus on sex
is so overwhelming that they often can't distinguish between a
woman expressing her natural affection and a woman wanting
sex. This is why men so often feel rejected. They'll read a
woman's signals incorrectly, believe the situation has moved on
to sex and then be faced with rejection. Women get equally
confused.

'You know, I often just want a cuddle before bed. I'd just like
us to be able to kiss each other and stroke each other to sleep.
Soft and gentle. It makes me feel good. But if I attempt that,
Robert always thinks I want sex. So now, as soon as I get into
bed, if I don't feel like sex, I pretend I'm asleep. I can't risk
snuggling up to him, because then he'll get an erection and
he'll want sex. Why can't he just cuddle? Why does sex have
to be so important?'   Helen

The problem for men is simply that they evolved with brain
hardwiring designed to keep the human species going. In
ancient times, they had to be ready to take every opportunity
to have sex, even in the face of danger. Often, pregnancies did-
n't make it to term and many babies died at birth or at an early

age. Most did not live into their teens. Women evolved with a lower sex drive because they had to take time out during pregnancy and to care for their children. If women wanted sex all the time, they might neglect their offspring in the search for sex or they would be constantly pregnant or giving birth. Both scenarios would be detrimental to their own health and that of their children.

Neanderthal man and woman apparently used to have no problem with sex – they thought it was just a bit of fun and probably never argued about the point of it. It was only when a more sophisticated kind of guy called Neolithic man came along that anyone made the connection between sex and childbirth. Before cheap, effective birth control became available, men had to try and suppress their sex drive or use the 'withdrawal' method to avoid being overrun by children.

Humans only recently made the connection between sex and childbirth.

3. How to Make Women Want Sex More Often

Historically, when men wanted something, they would ask in a direct way. When they didn't want something, they would also make that clear. Historically, men have always been in the position of being able to demand something and be given it. As the person who always held the power in a relationship, it often wouldn't occur to men to think any other way. As a consequence, many men still believe it's their right to demand sex. Today, women don't feel under any obligation to comply, and the more a man demands sex, the less likely they are to submit. Women don't understand why men don't try a more subtle approach, and men often don't even realise there is an alternative.

Today's women want to be made to feel sexy, loved, cherished and adored. They don't like to feel they are being taken

Four men went fishing. After an hour of sitting on the riverbank, one said, 'You won't believe what I had to do to get permission to come away fishing this weekend. I had to promise my wife that next week I'd redecorate every room in the house!'
The second man said, 'That's nothing! I had to promise my wife I'd turf the whole of the back garden and build swings and a slide for the kids.'
Man number three smiled. 'You don't know when you're well off!' he exclaimed. 'I had to promise my partner I'd renovate the whole of the kitchen for her and build a pergola in the garden!'
They continued to fish in silence. Then they realised the fourth man hadn't spoken.
'Hey, Jerry!' said the first man. 'What did you have to do to be able to come away fishing?'
Jerry shrugged casually. 'I just set my alarm for five thirty,' he said. 'When it went off, I turned it off, cuddled up to my wife and asked, "Fishing or sex?" She turned over and said, "Don't forget your jacket."'

for granted. And while foreplay is important, what happens before foreplay is even more important.

Stress has been found to be the biggest dampener of sexual desire in women because it creates negative emotions, and women's emotions are entwined with their desire for sex. If a woman is tired, fed up or anxious, then her sex drive can diminish to nothing, so it's important to help her feel relaxed, appreciated and needed.

Most men don't know that the biggest turn-on for women isn't the sight of an erect penis; it's more likely to be the sight of a man cooking dinner, doing the dishes, feeding the kids and putting his dirty clothes in the laundry.

These images are far more likely to make a woman feel tender towards a man than anything else. For a woman, particularly one with children or in a demanding job, it's hard to find the energy and inclination for sex when all she wants to do is sleep at the end of the day. A man getting involved in housework and domestic duties has been shown to be the best aphrodisiac he can offer a woman. Most men are stunned to hear that the sight of him vacuuming the house is a bigger turn-on than $300 spent at a fancy restaurant.

Maria Quinn, the author of *Between Clean Sheets*, a housework handbook for men, showed how housework and sex are intimately connected:

> *When a woman is running around and people expect so much of you, then sex becomes just another thing you have to give. It becomes something you – as a woman – do for someone else, rather than for yourself. Resentment builds up as you get more tired, uptight and angry about everything you have to do. A lot of men say, 'What am I doing wrong?' and they really don't know.*

Definitions of Foreplay
Hers: 'How about you clean the
kitchen while I soak in the bath tonight?'
His: 'Are you awake?'

Quinn says that a man taking on his share of the housework could then end up surprised by the unexpected outcome as the woman in his life suddenly becomes far more sexually demanding.

> **To want sex, women often want to feel needed, cherished, loved and adored first. Strangely, a man doing housework achieves this end.**

4. Why Women Have Orgasms

Only female humans have orgasms. For almost all other species, sex is a seven- to ten-second affair dedicated purely to procreation. No drawn-out bonding ritual is required. Human females have disguised ovulation – that is, a man never knows when she's 'on heat'. This appears to be an evolutionary adaptation designed to keep men around for most of the time. Women are almost always available for sex, whether they are ovulating or not, and this allows sex to become a constant bonding process, thus keeping men around.

Researchers inserted video cameras into the vaginas of women who were having an orgasm. The images reveal that at the moment of climax, the muscles of the vagina pull upward and the opening to the womb – the cervix – stretches forward and opens to draw up the sperm that is present, similar to the action of a vacuum-cleaner. This is why simultaneous orgasms between a man and a woman have special significance, as they increase the odds of conception. From a conception standpoint, female orgasm should only be during or after male ejaculation and not before.

Evolutionary biologists also see female orgasm as a form of quality control for the human species. They believe that if a woman senses that a man doesn't have the right genes she needs, her body is unlikely to go into orgasm mode. If, however, she goes off like a firecracker with him every night, it's Nature's way of telling her that, in evolutionary terms at least, he's got the genes she wants for her children.

5. Why Smart Women Are Often Fools In Love

Studies show that, in simple terms, the higher a woman's IQ (intelligence quota), the lower her EQ (emotional quota). This means that the brighter she is, the less likely she is to make good choices in love. Professional women, it has now been shown, are more likely to divorce and have affairs, and are less likely to have children. *The American Journal of Marriage and Family* cites several studies that show how the divorce rate rises for women who out-earn their male partners. In fact, women who earn more than their husbands divorce twice as often as those who earn less. It demonstrates that financially successful women are less tolerant and more controlling of less successful men and that these men have difficulty living with women who are more successful than them. Dr Robert Holden, author of *Success Intelligence*, says that intelligent women spend too much time analysing the meanings and motives in their relationships instead of just letting themselves be open and emotionally vulnerable to their men.

6. Why Women Prefer Older Men

David Buss found that women in all the 37 cultures he studied preferred older men. This is because the older a man is, the more likely he is to have greater resources and status. For example, the average earnings of an Australian male aged 20 in 2008 was $27,000, whereas a 30-year-old earned $44,000 and a 40-year-old made $53,000. Also, older men are more stable, more reliable and more likely to make a commitment. Women prefer men three to five years older because men who are significantly older are more likely to die, meaning their resources will end. In some cultures, women sometimes marry younger men, but this usually only happens when the woman is wealthy or if the man stands to inherit large amounts or will receive power and status. These marriages are usually 'arranged' marriages.

Men see women as sex objects. Women see men as success objects.

Occasionally, older women will get involved with much younger men and this happens for two reasons: first, she has her own resources and doesn't feel she needs a man's resources, and second, because older men mark her down on the Desirability Scale because she is past her child-bearing use-by date. She can attract a younger man by offering him sex or access to power and resources, but these relationships are almost always short-lived, as was the case with the then 59-year-old Elizabeth Taylor, who married 39-year-old construction worker Larry Fortensky.

Women prefer men who are more intelligent than themselves, and men prefer women who are less intelligent. You often see a dumb woman (or a woman playing dumb) with a smart man, but you'll rarely see a smart woman with a dumb man, other than in a comedy movie or a TV show attempting to portray irony or political correctness. It rarely happens in real life.

7. Why Women Want to Be Touched

In our book *Why Men Don't Listen & Women Can't Read Maps*, we revealed that women evolved over 10,000 touch receptors throughout their bodies, compared to 3,000 for men. Being sensitive to touch helped women assess the emotions and condition of their babies. It also explains why women love to be touched and why physical closeness is so important. For

A married couple in their mid-60s were celebrating their 35th wedding anniversary in a romantic little restaurant. Suddenly, a tiny fairy appeared on their table and said, 'For being a wonderful example to others of how to have a long, happy marriage, I will grant you each one wish.'

The wife squealed, 'We've always wanted to go on a world cruise!'

The fairy waved her magic wand and – poof! – two tickets for *The Queen Mary II* appeared in her hands.

The husband thought for a moment, then said, 'I'm sorry, my love, but an opportunity like this will never come again. My wish is to have a wife thirty years younger than me.'

His wife was very disappointed, but a wish is a wish. The fairy waved her magic wand and – poof! – the husband became 95 years old.

The moral of this story: men who are ungrateful bastards should remember that fairies are female.

most men, however, physical closeness is interpreted as meaning a woman wants sex, and this causes enormous relationship problems for couples everywhere. Women want plenty of non-sexual touching, such as cuddling, hand-holding, hair-stroking, massaging and any type of kissing. Most men do these things during the courtship phase with a woman because they know it could lead to sex, but many stop after the relationship becomes more permanent.

How do you know when a man is ready for sex? He's breathing.

8. Why Women Seem Distracted During Sex

Men everywhere complain that when it comes to having sex, women seem overly preoccupied with their surroundings. Men claim that women say the room is too light, too dark, too noisy, too quiet, that the walls are too thin or that someone will see them or hear them. Men are not concerned about these things – a man has a mono-tracking brain that focuses intently on the task at hand and he becomes virtually deaf and blind to outside stimuli.

> **'My wife always laughs during sex,
> no matter what she's reading.'**
> *Emo Phillips*

Neuroscientist Professor Gert Holstege of the University of Groningen in the Netherlands and his team compared the brain activity of 13 heterosexual women in 4 states: while resting, faking an orgasm, having their clitoris stimulated and clitoral stimulation to the point of orgasm. As the women were stimulated, activity rose in the primary somatosensory cortex, but fell in the amygdale and hippocampus (the brain regions involved in alertness and anxiety), confirming that women cannot enjoy sex unless they are relaxed and free from worries and distractions.

Women's multi-tasking brains can deal with all this data simultaneously. In ancient times, if a copulating couple both focused on their lovemaking, they could become targets for predators. Someone needed to be hardwired to keep guard, and women got the job.

To keep a woman in the mood, a man needs to pick the right time, to be sure she is stress-free, play soft music to cover up external sounds and assure her that she is safe and won't be disturbed.

9. How Women Perceive Sexual Aggression

Sexual aggression can be broadly defined as one person pushing their sexual urges on to another without permission. Dr David Buss listed 147 upsetting actions related to sex and found that women rated sexual aggression the worst possible act a man could perform in a relationship (93–100%). This is completely contrary to the image portrayed by Internet porn, which suggests that women have a strong urge to be involved in violent sex. If a woman dreams about having sex, it's usually with a rich, handsome man who is prepared to dedicate his resources to her – it's rarely sex with a rough, tough, unemployed loser with bad body odour. Men were less concerned about sexual aggression (43%), and some reported it would be a turn-on for them.

Buss also found that men consistently underestimate how acceptable sexual aggression is to women. The act men rated as the worst a woman could do was infidelity, closely followed by verbal aggression. Three-quarters of women, however, overestimated a man's response to aggression by her. It all means that most women are likely to reject a firm slap on the bum, whereas a man either doesn't mind doing it or thinks it's a good idea. In a world in which women believe that men think like women and men assume women think like men, we have a recipe for disaster.

10. How Women View Sexual Harassment

Of all complaints filed about sexual harassment, 93% are made by women and the remaining 7% are filed by men about harassment by other men. Occasionally there are complaints from men about sexual harassment from women, but these tend to have ulterior motives, such as one-upmanship or office politics, not sexual harassment. On the surface the statistics could easily show that almost all harassment is by men against women, but there are several mitigating factors: first, women experience a higher degree of stress about what they perceive to be harassment, and second, few men report being sexually harassed by a woman – men dream about it happening! For example, David Buss found that on a 7-point scale of excitement, when a woman rubs her body against a man in a bar he'll rate it 6.07. When a man does the same thing to a woman, she rates it as only 1.82, and this act is generally seen as a turn-off to many women.

Three out of four complaints by women are from women aged 20 to 35, further showing how a woman's child-bearing potential is the key attraction factor. A small minority of complainants are older women.

> **Most women take offence to sexual harassment by a man.**
> **Most men take sexual harassment by a woman as a compliment.**

Barbara Gutek, professor of psychology at the Claremont Graduate School in California, conducted a workplace study in which workers were asked for their reactions to a co-worker asking them to have sex. She found that 55% of women reported that they had been sexually harassed in the last 5 years, while only 9% of men were likely to have been sexually harassed by a woman in their working lives, and hardly any reported it. She also found that 63% of women would be insulted by a sex request versus 15% of men, and that 67% of men would feel flattered by the request versus 17% of women.

David Buss conducted another experiment in which he asked women to rate the degree of upset they would feel when approached by men from different status levels. Women were most offended by a request for sex by construction workers and rubbish collectors (60% were upset). The offence decreased as the man's occupation and potential for resources improved. Successful rock stars and college graduates caused offence to only 38% of women, demonstrating the difference a man's potential for resources plays in a woman's decision to have sex with him.

11. Why Women Fantasise About Bad, Bad Men

For most women, the attraction to bad boys usually happens over a two- to three-day period when she is ovulating. Her body craves the Russell Crowe bad-guy type because aggressive men have a greater survival rating than nice guys – and she wants his genes. As we said in *Why Men Don't Have a Clue & Women Always Need More Shoes*, dominant, high-testosterone males have always survived over the quiet, timid types, and on a primal level, this has an attraction to ovulating women. For the rest of the month, she's happy to settle for the quiet, reliable nurturing type.

While a woman consciously looks for a man who can provide support and will commit to her, she also wants a man who has good genes. Unfortunately, these two requirements don't always exist in one man. This is evidenced by current DNA tests, which reveal around 10% of babies born in wedlock are not the offspring of the husband. This has probably been the case for centuries but DNA testing has proved it.

In times of high stress, this phenomenon is amplified because the brain drives people to procreate in the face of their possible death. Hospital records in the UK reveal that during World War Two, one in six babies born in Britain in wedlock was not the child of the husband. The combination of wartime stress and the opportunities to mate with visiting US soldiers increased people's desire to procreate.

12. Why So Many Women Prefer Chocolate to Sex

For men, chocolate is just another food and not an addiction as it can be for so many women. Women with low serotonin levels are the most addicted chocoholics because phenylethy-lamine (PEA) – a feel-good chemical contained in chocolate – improves their feeling of well-being. Women eat more chocolate during their period than at most other times and chocolate is the number one choice for recovering heroin addicts. Chocolate's ingredients also attach to the cannaboid receptors in the female brain, meaning that when a woman eats it, she feels the combination of both falling in love and being high on marijuana.

Ten secret reasons women prefer chocolate to sex

1. Chocolate satisfies you even when it goes soft.
2. You can safely have chocolate while you're driving.
3. You can have chocolate anywhere (even in front of your mother).
4. You can have chocolate at any time of the month.
5. With chocolate there's no need to fake enjoyment.
6. The word 'commitment' doesn't frighten chocolate.
7. You can have chocolate on your desk and not upset your boss.
8. Having chocolate doesn't mean keeping the neighbours awake.
9. Chocolate doesn't keep you awake snoring after you've had it.
10. With chocolate, size doesn't matter.

Summary

It should be apparent to you by now that women do enjoy sex but for very different reasons to men. Women want to feel special, be respected, involved in decision-making and for their opinions to be valued. For men reading this information, if you treat women as if they are different to you in their perceptions of love and sex, you will discover a new world of female sexual response you could never have imagined.

- Understanding that men and women have different sexual needs and motivations is the key to a good sex life and a happy relationship.
- Women have evolved with a lower sex drive than men, as they needed to take time out from procreating to care for their young.
- Women need emotional input. If men want their partner to initiate sex more, they need to be loving, cherishing and do the washing-up: a stressed woman will place sex very low down on her priority list.
- Women do want sex, and more often than they care to admit.

Chapter 10
13 Tactics That Can Improve Your Mating Rating

Bob was popular. He was the only man in the nudist camp who could carry four coffees and ten doughnuts.

Eight Things Men Can Do to Improve Their Rating With Women

Throughout this book, we have shown you the primary motivations men and women have in relation to sex and love. Based on the surveys by the evolutionary psychologists and biologists mentioned in this book about what makes a man attractive to women, here's a collective summary of the things more than 20,000 women said were the most valuable steps a man can take to improve his Mating Rating.

1. Show commitment

Displaying commitment is a powerful attractant to women

because it implies a man's long-term potential to share his resources with her. The top signals women use to gauge a man's commitment are:

1 **Showing concern for her problems.** This demonstrates that his commitment may be there in times of need and that he will offer emotional support.

2 **Consistent courting.** Continually taking her out, buying flowers, phoning her, sending letters and sending texts or emails shows that he is a good long-term prospect and is less likely simply to want casual sex. Studies have shown that the more persistent a man is in courting a woman, the more likely she will be to marry him. The crucial part of constant courtship is that the woman being pursued must have at least a mild interest in the man. Persistent courting without her interest is seen as stalking.

2. Show self-confidence

In 1989, Barkow found that the level of a man's self-confidence is directly related to his income and, therefore, his resources, correlating with the studies that show that men with higher incomes have more casual sex partners. Several studies have also found that the higher a man's confidence, the more likely he is to approach attractive women in a club or bar. Faking confidence is also one of the tactics used by many men in an attempt to attract women, but most women are fairly good at detecting fakers. Setting clear goals to improve his abilities and resources increases a man's genuine self-confidence, and as a result, his body produces even more testosterone, which further increases his self-confidence. A man should set goals, have a variety of interests, get into shape physically and show he is ambitious.

3. Show kindness

Men who act compassionately towards a woman, show sensitivity to her needs and do helpful things for her indicate that they will be there for her in the long term and will direct resources to her. Most men whose goal is quick, short-term sex understand this and will fake kindness by acting more polite, considerate and compassionate than they really are. It is a tactic that men seeking casual sex will use. This is the man who is over the top with attention to a woman he has just met.

From a range of women's magazines, we collated the results of 53 surveys that asked women what they found attractive in a man. Other than fidelity, here are the top five:

1 Showing empathy and understanding
2 Listening
3 Displaying good manners
4 Caring
5 Offering help

These are also the least expensive tactics used by men to attract women into brief sexual encounters. Men looking for casual sex do so by feigning the things a woman looks for in a permanent partner and by acting out the virtues she wants in the 'right' man. Pretending to have long-term intentions only works well for men – women never use it.

4. Show off physical abilities

Many women understand that to attract a man, they need to make him feel strong, so they feign inability to carry a heavy bag, open a jar or kill a spider. When describing the men they are attracted to, 92% of women say they like a man with a well-developed chest and arms – in other words, he looks like an animal-catcher. Here in the 21st century, health clubs and gyms are full of men grunting and groaning and pumping iron in an attempt to make their bodies appear as if they are capable of catching animals and fighting enemies. A highly muscled male body has little real practical purpose nowadays, but men know that women admire this look. A set of perfectly defined abdominal muscles have no real functional value today other than for women to admire.

To attract women, men will instinctively display their hunting skills in things like sports, pressing weights, flexing their muscles, carrying heavy items and opening jars. Studies show that athletes have around double the casual sex that non-athletes have. So if you are a man, join a health club or start your own exercise regime and make yourself fit and strong. As we've said, lazy, fat guys shaped like an apple only get beautiful women in the movies – and movies are fiction. The fitter you are, the more your self-esteem and confidence will rise and the more high-quality mates you will attract.

My wife was standing in the kitchen, preparing our usual soft-boiled eggs and toast for breakfast, wearing only the T-shirt that she normally slept in. As I walked in, she turned to me and said softly, 'You've got to make love to me right now.'
My eyes lit up and I thought, I am either still dreaming or this is going to be my lucky day! Not wanting to lose the moment, I embraced her and then gave it my all, right there on the kitchen table.
'Thanks.' She sighed and returned to the stove, her T-shirt still round her neck.
Happy, but a little confused, I asked, 'What was that all about?'
'The egg-timer is broken,' she said.

5. Wearing powerful clothing

Anthropologists John Townsend and Gary Levy from Syracuse University conducted an experiment to demonstrate the power of expensive clothing as an attraction signal to women. They showed women photographs of men wearing hi-status clothing, such as three-piece suits, navy blazers, white shirts with designer ties and Rolex watches. The women were asked to rate their level of attraction to the men and how likely they would be to have coffee with each man, go on a date with him, have sex with him or marry him. The women were also shown pictures of the same men dressed in low-status clothing, such as T-shirts and jeans, singlets, baseball caps and a Burger King uniform. Overall, the women said they would consider having coffee, dating, having sex or marrying the men in the high-status clothing but would not consider doing the same with the men dressed in the low-status clothing. These results have been replicated in other cultures, producing the same results. The bottom line is that the hunter with the best hunting skills, the most cattle or best beads and bracelets gets the most women.

Elizabeth Hill, Elaine Nocks and Lucinda Gardner investigated the effects of both physique and clothing and jewellery status on the perceived attractiveness of males and females, using 81 female and 61 male college students. Physique display was manipulated by altering clothing tightness and skin exposure; status was manipulated with clothing changes representing the dress of different socioeconomic classes. Subjects provided ratings for opposite-sex models' physical, dating, sexual and marital attractiveness. All attractiveness measures were enhanced when models wore high-status clothing, primarily when physique was not also displayed. Accentuating the body produced an overall enhancement of attractiveness as a sexual partner but a decrease in attractiveness as a marital partner.

> **What's the difference between a man with a mid-life crisis and a circus clown?**
> **A circus clown knows he's wearing funny clothes.**

Men do not want to throw clothing away. They will still wear boxer shorts years after the elastic has died and they are only being held up by the crotch in his trousers. Many women have a simple clothing test – if you haven't worn an item in a year, throw it out. You've had it through all four seasons and haven't worn it, so toss it out, especially underwear. A man should ask his partner, sister, mother, neighbour or any other female friend to critique his wardrobe, and he should also give her full authority to dump anything that needs dumping.

6. Demonstrate caring

Evolutionary psychologists Peggy La Cerra, Leda Cosmides and John Tooby conducted an experiment in which they showed women images of a man displaying three different attitudes: standing alone, interacting positively with a baby and ignoring a baby in distress. The women rated the man who interacted with the baby as the most attractive and the man ignoring the baby as the least attractive. When men were shown images of women displaying the same attitudes towards babies, it made no difference to their attraction to her. When this experiment was carried out by other researchers using a puppy instead of a baby, it produced the same results in women's attraction to the man. Similarly, the men were equally attracted to the woman in each image, but some men remarked that even though the woman was attractive, she shouldn't be mean to the dog. To the baby, maybe, but never the dog. The bottom line for men here is clear: paying positive attention towards babies or to a woman's pet pays big dividends.

7. Show honesty

Displaying honesty was rated by women as being in the top 10% of tactics a man can use to obtain a long-term partner. Feigning it to get a short-term sexual relationship also works. A man who wants to impress a potential long-term partner should not exaggerate his resources or status. Telling a woman he runs a food-distribution business will backfire if in fact he is a pizza delivery man, but telling her he is starting at the bottom to learn the ropes so that he will one day own the pizza business is impressive. Being honest doesn't mean if a woman asks, 'Does my bum look big?' that you say, 'Yes.' It means that you tell her that you love her exactly how she is. Sure, if she lost a little weight you think she'd feel better, but it doesn't bother you at all.

> **Her: 'Does this dress make my bum look big?'**
> **Him: 'No, your bum makes that dress look big.'**

8. Displays of love

Any action that demonstrates love is seen as a sign of commitment. These include buying a special gift for her, showing loving behaviour – especially in front of others – and regularly saying, 'I love you.' Women rate the power of a display of love based on the amount of effort a man puts into it. Men often think of a display of love as doing something dramatic or expensive. For example, he sends a woman a huge bunch of flowers or takes her to an expensive restaurant and leaves a big tip. These acts definitely earn points for a man, but over the longer term his effort is the key. If he makes her life easier by doing the housework, washing the dishes or babysitting the kids so that she has time to have a stress-free massage or enjoy a facial, he'll score big time. The effort he expends is more important than what he can buy. A handwritten note from him saying how special she is beats a £20 note on any field.

How Men Criticise the Competition

A man who wants to run down the Mating Rating of a competitor can do it by inferring to a woman that the competitor has little ambition, no motivation, lousy assets and couldn't lead a group in silent prayer. In other words, he belittles the competitor's potential to gain power or gather resources. He can also diminish a rival's attractiveness by stating or implying that the rival is promiscuous and can't stay loyal to one woman – meaning that he would be spreading his resources far and wide and not channelling them into her. He might say that the competitor has a steady girlfriend and/or children, indicating that he would have fewer resources to direct towards a potential new mate. This approach only works because women are hardwired to select men who have resources or the potential to get them. He doesn't say the other man is ugly or losing his hair, because these things are low-ranking on women's desire list. This is why men exaggerate the criteria that are important to women: they lie to women about jobs, salaries, status and level of commitment to try to increase their Mating Rating.

Five Things Women Can Do to Increase Their Mating Rating

Based on the surveys of what over 20,000 men said, here's a collective summary of the most valuable actions women can take to improve their attractiveness and their Mating Rating.

1. Enhance and improve appearance

We surveyed magazine stands in 24 countries and found that they advertise the same stories and images everywhere. In priority order, here are the main cover stories promoted in women's magazines:

1 How to enhance your appearance

2 How to give/get better sex
3 Stories about someone's relationship/health/appearance
4 Food – either cooking it or dieting
5 Tests and quizzes to assess relationship suitability with a man

Women are shown how to enhance their appearance to get more love and sex, but then magazines also have pages teaching them how to prepare food that make them lose sight of these same objectives by gaining weight.

Compare these stories to men's magazine cover stories, which show:

1 How to build muscles
2 How to improve virility
3 How to get more casual sex
4 Spatial- and testosterone-related stories – fishing, computers, hunting, sports, cars and careers.

Because men place such importance on a woman's appearance, women strive to make themselves appear reproductively more valuable by displaying youth, health and physical attractiveness. Women spend 3 times as much time as men on their physical appearance and 15 times as much on products to maintain that appearance. Women who fail to do this lose their edge in the mating game. Even though some men now use a range of cosmetics, it is usually limited to aftershaves, skin conditioners and hair products. A man spending too much time on his appearance can be seen by women as egotistical or that he could be gay, which reduces his attractiveness to women.

Almost all deceptive visual aids are used by women to attract men. These include wearing high heels to make the legs appear longer (higher fertility), artificial nails to make the hands look longer, breast implants to look more youthful, dark clothing or vertical stripes to appear thinner, dying their hair, cosmetic surgery, wearing wigs and padding their clothing.

In the 19th century, many of these tactics were illegal and a woman could be jailed for using them to attract a man.

The reason these strategies work is because they are from the preferences hardwired into male brains. It's not that women necessarily want to do these things, it's because men want them to and women know it.

> **A beggar walked up to a well-dressed woman shopping on Rodeo Drive and said, 'I haven't eaten anything in four days.' She looked at him and said, 'Man, I wish I had your willpower.'**

Cosmetic surgery and the cosmetics industry target women's need to enhance their appearance and look healthy and youthful to men. Face powder evens out the skin and hides any evidence of potential health problems, and a facelift removes the signs of low fertility. Lipsticks and collagen injections enlarge the lips, and shades of red mimic increased bloodflow, which signals a woman may be sexually receptive. Mascara gives the illusion that a woman's eyes are wider and receptive to males, and hair shampoos and conditioners suggest that her recent health has been excellent. Men see flushed cheeks as a sign of good health in women, so women use blushers to feign health. Because men are attracted to youthful, perky breasts, women wear push-up bras or have breast implants. Women who do these things claim it is 'to feel better about themselves'. The truth is that they feel better about themselves because men are more attracted to them. Women's magazines promote cover pictures of women displaying the health and youth cues to which women aspire, while men's magazines show younger women displaying these same cues plus using body-language gestures and positions that indicate sexual availability. The only time that men are shown on the cover of men's magazines is when the story is about how a man can enhance his appearance by building his body so he can look as if he could wrestle a large animal.

2. Highlight fidelity

Dr David Buss identified 130 tactics of attraction among people from 22 cultures. Here are the top three he reported that men wanted from women:

1. Faithfulness
2. Avoiding sex with other men
3. Showing devotion

These were ranked by men as at least 93% important for a woman to have as they were strong indicators of a man's paternity. Ancestral men had no way of knowing whether a child was really theirs, but they had a harem of women, so a man's odds of bearing his own children were good. The above three characteristics would be more important to the 21st-century man than to his ancestors because today's women now insist on monogamy. This means a man is limited to one woman to carry his genes forward, so he needs better guarantees of his paternity.

As we revealed earlier, it's only since DNA testing has become common that it has been shown that in the UK, for example, 1 baby born in 11 within marriage is *not* the child of the husband. This is why saying that a rival cannot stay faithful to one man has been shown to be one of the most effective tactics a woman can use. The catch here is that this tactic only works on a man who is looking at a woman from a long-term standpoint. Considering a man's short-term list for casual sex, saying a woman is loose or sleeps around actually elevates her in his estimation.

The fact that men detest female promiscuity in long-term partners has given rise to at least 100 words over the last 1,000 years to describe a promiscuous woman, most of which are derogatory. There are few – if any – negative words used to describe promiscuous male behaviour, and these words are usually used with a sense of pride or envy. Some words used for women include tramp, slapper, slut, harlot, whore, wench, strumpet, nut-cracker, meat-grinder, hussy, prostitute, moll, streetwalker, loose woman, tart, ho, concubine, hooker, lady of the night, bike, call girl, trollop, scrubber, skank, nympho, groundsheet and slag.

Now here are some words used for men – sex god, stud, sex addict, player, cock-hound, cocksman, playboy, rooster, cowboy, swordsman, sausage pilot, macho man, root rat, Casanova, bonkmaster, pussy-pounder, sausage-stuffer, gigolo, pussy-puncher, pants man, muff magnet, stallion, womaniser, stud muffin, shag-happy and ram. Most of these words are directly or indirectly complimentary to men.

The three best ways for women to highlight fidelity are:

1 Don't talk about men in your past relationships.
2 Don't flirt with other men.
3 Don't have sex early in a new relationship. Early means before he has demonstrated that he is prepared to invest his resources and time into you.

3. Play hard to get

Acting shy, bashful or coy were also found to be very effective when used by women on men who were seeking a long-term partner. Coyness works on men as it indicates that a woman could be hard to get and is seen as an indicator of fidelity. If a woman is an 'easy lay', a man assumes that she'll also be easy for other men, which compromises his certainty of paternity. Playing hard to get is an excellent strategy as it appeals to two primitive male motivations of men: fidelity and assurance that his kids are really his.

People everywhere are deeply interested in the sexual reputation of others, and because of these motivations, talk shows such as *Jerry Springer*, *Ricki Lake*, *Maury Povich* and *Jeremy*

> **'Am I the first man ever to make love to you?' he asked.**
> **'You could be,' she said. 'You look kind of familiar.'**

Kyle centre on them – who is sleeping with who, how often, why, when and where, and who's the father? For men seeking a casual sex partner, however, coyness is a negative as it indicates that too much hard work or resources would be needed on his part. A woman who withholds sex raises her Mating Rating because it forces a man to look at her as a potential long-term partner.

> **Giving in to sex early causes a man to perceive a woman as a casual partner.**

4. Show less skin

Nocks, Hill and Gardner showed men and women a series of images of the opposite sex in which varying amounts of skin were exposed. The more skin a woman showed, the higher men rated her as a potential casual sex partner but the lower they rated her as a long-term partner. The tighter-fitting and more revealing the woman's clothing was, the higher she rated as a short-term sex partner and the lower as a marriage partner.

Women rated men in less dress and more revealing clothing as short-term mates, and fully clothed men rated higher as marriage partners. The lower the cut of a woman's dress and the more she revealed of her boobs, the less the men could remember – or cared – about anything she said.

The lesson here is that the more skin a woman has covered – especially in erotic areas – the more likely she is to be perceived as a potential long-term partner.

5. Act dumb, helpless or submissive

Dr Buss found that these three tactics work reasonably well in attracting short-term mates (48% effective) but not so good for attracting long-term partners (23% effective). The key to these tactics is that they imply that a man with short-term motives is less likely to be rejected by a woman who acts dumb, helpless or submissive, and he may easily be able to manipulate her. This explains the history of the 'dumb blonde'.

How Women Criticise the Competition

When a woman wants to run down a competitor's Mating Rating, she criticises her health and beauty. She could infer that the competitor has fake breasts, has had a facelift, has a sexually transmittable disease or sleeps around. Again, these ploys only work because men's brains are hardwired to seek out health, youth and fidelity. She would never say that her competitor had a lousy job and didn't own her own home. When it comes to exaggeration, women lie to men about their age (youth), how many lovers they've had (fidelity) and their health (cosmetics, high heels, plastic surgery and so on).

Because men place such a premium on a woman's appearance, women not only strive to improve their own appearance, they belittle the physical appearance of their rivals. They denigrate competitors by saying they are fat, ugly, shapeless or unattractive: 'Have you seen her without her make-up?' and 'She's got fake boobs/lips/too much make-up.' You'll never hear a woman say that a competitor has no ambition or owns a crap car. Criticising another woman's faithfulness only works on a man who is looking at a woman as a long-term prospect. If you call a woman a slut, she immediately becomes more attractive to men seeking casual sex.

**To be happy with a man, you must understand him a lot and love him a little.
To be happy with a woman, you must love her a lot and not try to understand her at all.**

- It is possible to improve your Mating Rating with the opposite sex.
- Men should be empathetic and supportive of the woman in their life. Little displays of commitment and affection mean a lot more to a woman than big, expensive gifts.
- Women should highlight their fidelity, avoid showing too much flesh and focus on their appearance if they want to improve their Mating Rating.
- Both men and women will actively criticise the competition in order to bring down their Mating Rating. Men criticise other men's resources, or ability to get them, while women attack other women's appearance.

Chapter 11
A Happier Future Together?

Whatever our age, when we are in love we are teenagers. The new woman wants the thrill of love, romance, adventure, sexual passion and to be a free, independent person. Her dream is to find a man who loves her and will allow her to do these things. The new man wants what men have always wanted – to be admired, respected, understood and for his partner to be faithful. And if it wasn't financially necessary for her to work, he wouldn't want her to.

Feminists usually take the standpoint that men have controlled the world's resources for thousands of years and controlled women by getting them pregnant, thus preventing them from obtaining their own power and resources. When you study our history, this argument certainly appears to be true – at first. But standing back and looking at the big picture of the human species raises an important question – why did men evolve with the urge to gather resources, status and power? The answer is that women evolved as child-bearers and wanted mates who had the resources required to feed and protect their children. On a subconscious level, most men know this, which is why they spend their lives in the pursuit of the status and resources to meet females' requirements. Why else would men everywhere knock themselves out and ruin their health to compete with other men for better jobs, higher status and bigger salaries? They do it because they understand that if they can beat other men in the status and resource game, they will attract mates of a higher quality. If men didn't need to mate with women, there would be no urgency to meet the resource criteria set by women. Men would choose a less stressful life and go fishing, drink beer, sleep in and fart anytime they wanted.

Today, women everywhere continue to seek men who have resources or who display the potential to gather these resources. Women reject men who have no resources or who have little ambition to attain them. Some people are quick to point out a couple in which the woman is the driver for resources and the man is a laid-back, stay-at-home type, but these couples are the small minority.

Men who marry earn more money than men of the same age who do not marry.

Some feminists claim that the main objective of men is to oppress women. The reality is that men compete with other men for power, status and resources, not with women. Men compete against other men for the available women, and men use women's criteria preferences as their measurement of success at the resource game. Not only do men die seven years earlier than women in these pursuits, most murders involve men killing other men over matters of the heart.

Imagine if men responded the same way to women's need to bond and use talk as social glue. Imagine a man saying, 'You talk with your friends for hours on the phone – don't you love me any more? Don't you think I'm good enough to talk to?' or, 'You never take me shoe shopping – you always take Josephine. You only want me for sex!'

Unfortunately, men are vilified because of their natural urges, while women are praised for theirs under the flag of being 'wonderful communicators'. If all things were equal, men should be praised for being 'wonderful procreators'.

Not surprisingly, 76% of men deny that they are thinking about a woman sexually, mainly because they are afraid of criticism from women, being accused of sexual harassment or because they are being 'politically correct'.

Married People Are Now the Minority

Is marriage dead? If you are married, you are now in a minority. Married couples, whose numbers have been declining for decades as a proportion of Western households, slipped into a minority in 2006 in the US. The *American Community Survey*, released by the US Census Bureau, found that 49.7%, or 55.2 million, of America's 111.2 million households were made up of married couples – with and without children – down from more than 52% just 5 years earlier. With more competition from other ways of living, the proportion of married couples has been shrinking for decades. In 1930, they accounted for about 84% of households. By 1990, the proportion of married couples had declined to about 56%. The survey did not ask about sexual orientation, but its questionnaire was designed to distinguish partners from roommates.

In the UK, common-law partnerships outnumbered legally married couples in 2008 according to the Office for National Statistics. Between 1998 and 2007, the number of adults registered as married dropped by 8%, and in 2007 less than half of women aged between 18 and 49 were married, compared with almost 75% of those surveyed in 1979. Three times more women were unmarried in 2007 than in 1979. In 2006, only 236,980 weddings took place in England and Wales, the biggest dip in marriages since 1895. Marriage has been facing more competition than ever with a growing number of adults spending more of their lives single or living with partners.

Couples decide to live together for many reasons, but given the difficulty of finding an affordable home, practicality can be as important as romance because two people can live together more cheaply than one. Many couples today also say that cohabiting is like taking a relationship test drive.

Whatever the future brings, loving someone and being loved will always be vital to human survival. A study was conducted over 9 years by medical researchers in California of 7,000 men and women. The researchers found that those who lacked contact with friends, relatives, community, group membership, lovers or spouse were 1.9 to 3.1 times more likely to have died during that period. A similar study in Sweden tracked 17,000 men and women over a 6-year period and revealed that those who felt isolated or lonely were 4 times more likely to have died during that period, regardless of their race, sex or exercise habits.

Are Today's Youth More Informed?

One survey in the UK revealed that 80% of teenagers lose their virginity when they are drunk or feel pressured into having sex, and over half are having unprotected sex. The survey of 3,000 school pupils aged 15–18 found that 39% had sex for the first time when one or other partner was not equally willing. Almost three in ten lost their virginity for 'negative reasons', such as wanting to please a boyfriend. Furthermore, 51% of girls and 37% of boys had had unprotected sex, while 58% of girls and 39% of boys had slept with someone at least once without using a condom. These statistics reveal the depth of ignorance that lead many teenagers into having unsafe sex.

Evidence from the studies of children from divorced homes show that children will use the same mate-seeking strategies for their partners as their parents did. Where parents separate, children learn that you cannot depend on a single partner for life. They reach puberty sooner, girls menstruate younger, and teenagers have sex earlier with more partners than their peers whose parents remained together.

'Aren't you being just a little over-cautious?'

All these factors mean that today's youth may be more informed in some areas of sex than their parents but they have a less responsible attitude to safety and are more prepared to risk pregnancy, STDs or AIDS than their parents ever were.

Why New Love Always Seems So Promising

Our past has hardwired us to be attracted to mates with whom we can produce stronger offspring, just as it is for other animal species. This is why you can sometimes find yourself attracted to someone who has none of the criteria on your wish list. Just because you can produce good offspring doesn't mean you can live happily ever after. This is why a man will use tried and tested phrases to convince a woman that she's the only one for him – 'I've never felt about another woman like this' and 'We have a deep spiritual connection.' It is important for a woman to understand that the man who says these things early in a relationship often believes he means them at the time because his body chemicals are pushing him to do or say whatever is needed to get her knickers down. Her brain chemicals are convincing her to believe his lines, and her lie detector is usually switched off. Sure, go for the ride and enjoy the fun of early love, but remember that it's emotionally safer to expect a less permanent outcome than seems to be promised at the time. Unless a man has decided he wants a permanent relationship, a woman is simply the prey and he's the hunter. Most men enter a new relationship not expecting it to be long term. The man wants a woman to meet his basic needs and keep giving him his chemical rushes. And if his brain stops doing that, he'll swap, trade or upgrade her for another model.

We Are Definitely Different

There are now mountains of evidence showing how men and women think and behave differently. The following are further evidence of these behavioural variations.

How to shower like a woman

1. Take off clothing and place it in a sectioned laundry hamper according to lights, darks, whites, man-made or natural.
2. Walk to bathroom wearing long dressing gown. If husband seen along the way, cover up any exposed flesh and rush to the bathroom.
3. Look at womanly physique in the mirror and stick out belly.
4. Complain and whine about getting fat.
5. Get in shower.

6. Look for facecloth, body cloth, long loofah, wide loofah and pumice stone.

7. Wash hair once with cucumber and avocado shampoo with 83 added vitamins.

8. Wash hair again with cucumber and avocado shampoo with 83 added vitamins.

9. Condition hair with cucumber and avocado conditioner with enhanced natural orange-blossom oil. Leave on hair for 15 minutes.

10. Wash face with crushed-apricot facial scrub for ten minutes until red raw.

11. Wash entire rest of body with ginger-nut and Jaffa Cake body wash.

12. Rinse hair, taking at least 15 minutes to make sure that conditioner is all off.

13. Shave armpits and legs. Consider shaving bikini area but decide to get it waxed instead.

14. Scream loudly when husband flushes toilet and water loses pressure and goes red hot.

15. Turn off shower.

16. Squeegee all wet surfaces in shower.

17. Spray mould spots with Exit Mould.

18. Get out of shower.

19. Dry with towel the size of small African country.

20. Wrap hair in super-absorbent second towel.

21. Check entire body for remotest sign of spots. Attack with nails/tweezers if found.

22. Return to bedroom wearing long dressing gown and towel on head. If husband is seen, cover up any exposed areas and then rush to bedroom to spend an hour and a half getting dressed.

How to shower like a man

1. Take off clothes while sitting on the edge of the bed and leave them in a pile.

2.   Walk naked to the bathroom. If wife seen along the way, shake penis at her, making the 'woo-woo' sound.
3.   Look at manly physique in the mirror and suck in gut. Admire size of penis and scratch butt.
4.   Get in shower.
5.   Don't bother to look for washcloth.
6.   Wash face.
7.   Wash armpits.
8.   Blow nose in hands, then let water rinse it off.
9.   Crack up at how loud farts sound in shower.
10. Majority of time is spent washing privates and surrounding area.
11. Wash butt, leaving butt hairs on the soap bar.
12. Shampoo hair. (Do not use conditioner.)
13. Make a shampoo mohawk.
14. Peek out of shower curtain to look at self in mirror again.
15. Pee in shower, aiming for drainage hole.
16. Rinse off and get out of shower. Fail to notice water on floor because curtain hanging out of tub the whole time.
17. Partially dry off.
18. Look in mirror. Flex muscles. Admire penis size again.
19. Leave shower curtain open, wet bathmat on floor, fan and light on.
20. Return to bedroom with towel round waist. Pull off towel, shake penis at wife, go, 'Yeah, baby,' and thrust pelvis at her.
21. Throw wet towel on bed. Put on yesterday's clothes.

Do Opposites Really Attract?

The old cliché 'opposites attract' has likely caused more trouble and break-ups among men and women than any other. It infers that a couple will be attracted to each other if the woman likes tidiness but the man throws his clothes on the floor, if he's addicted to football but she can't stand it, if she loves art galleries while he loves discos, and if he's a teetotaller while she's near alcoholic. All studies that track the behaviour, attitudes and longevity of couples show clearly that while opposites certainly have some attraction value in the initial stages of attraction, it's a recipe for long-term tension and break-ups. Couples who differ in their base similarities and values are headed for divorce.

This is not to say that all couples who have many opposing characteristics and ideals won't last – a small minority do – but for most opposites, their lives are continually dogged by arguments and disagreements. This makes their joint progress towards any mutual goals slow and cumbersome. When couples have different life goals, they waste valuable time by continually going in opposite directions. David Buss found that the couples who experience the most successful long-term relationships and suffer the least number of break-ups are those who are similar in race, religion and ethnicity and who hold similar values or views on social, moral, ethical and political ideals.

The key, then, to successful long-term partnerships is to search for a mate with similar ideals and values. In other words, find someone who is like you in their core values and beliefs.

The World's Worst Lovers

So which men in the world are seen as the best lovers and who are the worst? In 2005, Bayer Healthcare released a report called 'Sex and the Modern Woman', which surveyed 12,065 women aged over 40 from 16 countries about their level of sexual satisfaction from their men. The countries included Brazil, France, Germany, Italy, Mexico, Poland, Saudi Arabia, South Africa, Spain, Turkey, the UK, Australia and Venezuela. Few people can guess who rated as the most sexually satisfied women. It was Saudi Arabian women, followed by Mexican,

Spanish, Italian and Venezuelan women. Saudi Arabian women are the most fulfilled and the most satisfied overall (92%) and have the greatest overall number in the survey reporting that they are 'very satisfied' (64%). Almost all of the Saudi Arabian women believe that their partner's sexual satisfaction is also 'essential' or 'important' (97%). Turkish women are least satisfied overall (65%), with just 32% very satisfied with their sex lives.

Saudi women are the world's most sexually satisfied women.

Dr John Dean, a consultant to the study, said that in Saudi and most other Arab societies, sex plays a very important part in marriage; it is a gift to enjoy, and husband and wife have a duty to share it. In the Muslim world in general, sex is reserved to married couples. In the Koran, men are commanded that women are to be respected and their needs are to be fulfilled and that spending time in advance is important. The Koran says, 'Let not the one of afore you fall upon his wife like a camel falls. It is more appropriate to set a messenger act.' Another instruction to men states, 'Women have rights even as they have obligations in an equitable way.' Saudi Arabian women affirm the importance of sex. They want fulfilling sex and are also prepared to give it to their husbands.

How Women In Other Countries View Sex

The women who said they were the most satisfied also rated sex highly in their lives. In Latin America, 92% of women rate their partner's satisfaction as 'essential' or 'important', while 91% rate their own satisfaction in the same way, and 82% of Venezuelan women rated sex as important in their lives. Mexican women give the next highest rating, with 80% of women stating that sex is 'important' to them.

Only 61% of women in the UK stated that sex is 'important' in their lives, and just 13% of French women felt the same. Around 30% of German women believe that sex is either 'not very important' or 'not important at all' in their lives, while 32% of Turkish women felt the same way.

Spontaneity in sex was rated as either 'essential' or 'important' for 92% of Italian women – Poland was a close second at 91% – but only 18% of UK women saw spontaneity in their sex lives as 'essential'. This was the lowest figure overall.

French women most want an improvement to their sex lives (37%), with 26% 'sometimes' wishing for an improvement. Italian women appear more satisfied, with only 4% often wanting an improvement and 14% 'sometimes' wanting it.

Who Is Missing Out?

The least satisfied women in the Western World were Australian women, with 33% saying their sex lives were 'not very' or 'not at all' satisfying, compared with a global female average of just 16%. Only 26% of Australian women rated their sex life 'very satisfying', and 36% were 'somewhat happy'.

A similar poll by social networking site WAYN.com quizzed 10,000 women in 50 countries about who they thought were the best lovers and what they didn't like about the men from various countries. The survey found that German men were considered the worst lovers in the world because they were too selfish. Second place went to Swedish men, who are too quick, with Dutch men in third place because they are too rough. Americans (too dominant) were fourth, followed by Welsh men (too soppy), Scots (too loud) and Turks (too sweaty). English men were tenth (too fat), followed by Greeks, who were too smelly, then Russians, who were too hairy. The best lovers were Italians and French.

> **A woman meets a man in a bar. They talk, they connect, and leave together. They get back to his apartment and she notices that his bedroom is completely packed with sweet, cuddly teddy bears. There are hundreds of cute small bears on a shelf on the floor, cuddly medium-sized ones on a shelf a little higher, and huge enormous bears on the top shelf.**
>
> **She is surprised that this man would have such a wonderful collection of teddy bears and is very impressed by his sensitive side. She turns to him, they kiss, and then they make hot, steamy love.**
>
> **After an intense night of passion with this sensitive man, they are lying together basking in the afterglow. She rolls over and asks, 'Well, how was it for you?'**
>
> **He replies, 'Help yourself to any prize on the bottom shelf.'**

Put Your Finger On Your Sex Drive and Success

Science has finally come up with its own answer to palm-reading. Studies now show that everything from sporting prowess to academic ability, and sexual orientation to susceptibility to disease can be assessed by your finger length.

Here's a hands-on experiment you can try right now. Hold your hand in front of your face and try to keep your fingers absolutely straight. Now notice the difference in length, if any, between your index finger and your ring finger. The ratio between your index finger and ring finger has been shown to be linked to exposure to the male hormone testosterone in the womb.

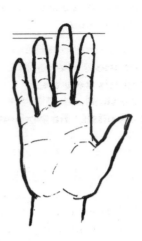 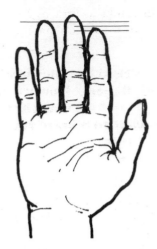

Typical female-finger ratio   Typical male-finger ratio

On average, men tend to have longer ring fingers than women, who have longer index fingers. The higher your testosterone, the greater the length of the ring finger and the more 'masculine' any baby born with this ratio will be, regardless of whether it's male or female.

It has been known for some time that people with longer ring fingers tend to excel on the sports field, especially in running and football, and science now shows why – the ring finger has a greater number of testosterone receptors than the others. The index finger has a larger number of oestrogen receptors. A high level of testosterone is what drives people into certain professions, is responsible for sexual orientation and determines your sex drive.

A person with an index finger shorter than the ring finger will have had more testosterone while in the womb, whereas a person with an index finger longer than the ring finger will have received more oestrogen. These studies throw light on why women who have a longer index finger are more likely to be more fertile than women who don't. The difference in the lengths can be as little as 2–3%, but it makes a significant difference to someone's masculinity or femininity.

> **'Hold up your hand and show me your fingers,' Ivor instructed his new date. 'But why?' she asked. 'I want to admire your nail polish,' he replied.**

In 2007, Dr Mark Brosnan at the University of Bath tested 100 men and women, and found that longer index fingers indicated good verbal and literacy skills. These are the brain skills that are dominated by females. Brosnan also found that children – both male and female – who had longer ring fingers are better with maths and physics than those with the opposite finger ratio. They also concluded that a longer ring finger for boys may be an indicator of autism, which is four times more common in boys than girls, and that these boys could be at greatest risk of a heart attack in early adulthood. Lesbian women have been shown to be more likely to have longer ring fingers, indicating exposure to higher levels of testosterone when they were in the womb.

Professor John Manning, author of *The Finger Book*, said the ratio was decided during the early period of pregnancy and was a measure of exposure to testosterone and oestrogen, and is thereby an indicator of a person's future potential. He conducted research on gay men that showed that gays were more likely to have the same finger ratios as women, showing that they had received less testosterone in the womb.

In 2008, John Coates and colleagues at Cambridge University measured the right hands of 44 male London stock traders and took saliva samples from them in the mornings and evenings. They monitored the traders over 20 months and found that those with longer ring fingers compared to their index fingers made 11 times more money than those with the shortest ring fingers. Over the same time, the most experienced traders made about nine times more than the least experienced ones. Looking only at experienced traders, the long-ring-finger traders earned five times more than those with short ring fingers. They also found that those with higher levels of testosterone in the morning were more likely to make a big profit that day. They believe that the finger ratio appears to signal the likely success in high-actively trading, which calls for risk-taking and quick reactions, because testosterone affects aggression, confidence and risk-taking.

The Science of Future Love

Science will likely play a significant part in how we will love in the future.

Genetic studies of mating and courtship have so far remained limited to animals and to relatively simple questionnaires. The most spectacular study of this type was conducted with two species of North American voles, which are a type of rodent. These are the monogamous prairie voles and the genetically related montane voles, which do not form any bonds but bonk every vole in sight. Researchers Thomas Insel and Larry Young at Emory University in Atlanta, Georgia, discovered a gene in the monogamous prairie vole that is absent in the polygamous montane vole. They incorporated the gene into the male montane voles. This simple genetic manipulation succeeded in 'curing' these rodents of their promiscuity. It will soon be possible to genetically modify people to make them monogamous or to turn them into raving sex maniacs.

> **Marriage and love are purely a matter of chemistry. That is why one often treats the other like toxic waste.**

Sniffing Out a Good Partner

Scientists who study genetics and mate preferences have shown that each of us is attracted to people who possess a particular set of genes, known as the major histocompatibility complex (MHC). The MHC is a gene family that makes molecules that enable the immune system to recognise invaders. The more diverse the MHC genes of the parents, the stronger the immune system of the offspring. In 1995, Claus Wedekind, professor of biology at the University of Lausanne, Switzerland, conducted the famous 'sweaty T-shirt' experiment, which showed how we unconsciously select mates with dissimilar MHC to us. He asked a group of women to smell T-shirts that men had worn for two nights, without deodorant, cologne or soap. The shirts were then put into identical boxes. The women were asked to smell the shirts and to indicate which shirts they were most sexually attracted to. Overwhelmingly, the women preferred the odours of men with dissimilar MHCs to their own. Another study in 2002 showed how we mainly use smell to detect a person's MHC.

However, if they were taking oral contraceptives, their preference was reversed. In 2005, a study of 58 women taking the Pill confirmed that using oral contraceptives made women prefer men with MHCs similar to their own. The women in the experiment who were not taking oral contraceptives had no particular preference. This shows how a woman taking the Pill can make the opposite partner choice to her natural instinct. These studies confirm that people literally appear to sniff out their mates' pheromones and that women prefer the odour of physically symmetrical men. This is what 'sexual chemistry' is all about. You'll know it's happened to you when you meet someone and for no explicable reason find yourself excited by their presence.

Your perfect match could be right under your nose.

Race differences apply to MHC detection. In 2008, Professor Peter Donnelly, director of Oxford University's Wellcome Trust Centre for Human Genetics, and colleagues showed that MHC is related to mating choice in European Americans but not in Africans.

Drugs and other treatments are being developed that can cause people to fall in and out of love and to recover more easily from lost love, so what does the future hold for love? Greater knowledge of something very often brings with it the ability to manipulate and control it. People will be able to immunise themselves from love by using treatments that prevent the lust or romantic love processes from developing in the first place. A person with a poor track record in relationships might decide that the possibility of a new love is just too painful to bear and might want to protect themselves from romantic distractions to devote their time to a career. Or they could decide that love is just too costly and they are better off without it. Or they might try getting rid of their mate by secretly feeding them a compound that makes them fall out of love...or fall in love with you.

For love and lovers, the future holds things that have so far only been seen in the movies.

Ten Reasons Why Sex Is Good Medicine

1. Sex cures mild depression by releasing endorphins into the bloodstream, producing a sense of euphoria and a feeling of well-being.
2. Sex is a natural antihistamine. It can help combat asthma and hay fever. No one ever gets a stuffy nose during lovemaking.
3. Lovemaking can burn up those calories you piled on during that romantic dinner.
4. Sex tones up just about every muscle in the body, and it's more fun than swimming 20 lengths.
5. When women make love, they produce large amounts

of oestrogen, which makes hair shiny and skin smooth.

6. The more often you have sex, the more sex you will be offered. A sexually active body secretes large quantities of pheromones. These subtle sex perfumes drive the opposite sex crazy.

7. Sex is around ten times more effective as a tranquilliser than Valium.

8. Kissing encourages saliva to wash food from the teeth and lowers the level of the acid that causes decay and plaque build-up.

9. Sex relieves headaches by releasing the tension that restricts blood vessels in the brain.

10. Gentle, relaxed lovemaking reduces your chance of suffering dermatitis, rashes and blemishes. The sweat produced cleanses the pores and makes the skin glow.

How So Many Were Fooled

The politically correct lobby still continues to staunchly resist the overwhelming evidence that we are born with inherent brain differences that dictate our choices and preferences. Any parent who is raising both a boy and a girl quickly realises you can give sons and daughters equal love, equal opportunity, equal everything and you will still get a completely different response. Give a teddy bear to both a three-year-old boy and girl, and the girl will nurture the bear, give it a name and make it her best friend. The boy will sit it on a fence, throw things at it, pull it apart to see how it's put together, then walk away leaving a mess behind. While a girl patiently watches a bird singing in a tree, her brother tries to hit it with a rock. The parents never taught their children to behave like this – they are hardwired in the womb to do it. And so men will still ogle any big-breasted woman who wiggles past, and women will do the same to any well-built man with a gold watch, a tight bum, a nice smile and a fancy car.

A man is no longer said to have a 'beer gut' or get lost when he's driving; he now has a 'liquid grain storage facility' and 'investigates alternative destinations'.

He's not a 'balding old fart' who is a 'cradle-snatcher'; he's now a person with 'follicle regression' who prefers 'generationally different relationships'.

A woman is no longer called an 'airhead with big hooters' who has 'been around'; she's now a 'reality-impaired breasted individual' who is a 'previously enjoyed companion'.

Who Gets Who?

In life, there is only a small percentage of highly attractive potential partners. These attractive people are desired by the majority of people, who, in fact, do not have a high Mating Rating themselves. That's why most people settle for partners who have roughly the same Mating Rating as themselves. Most people do not recognise the minor everyday things they do as being part of an urge to compete successfully for mates. For example, few women consider that buying a face cream that helps remove wrinkles, or a lipstick that highlights the lips, or a conditioner to make the hair shine are all designed to try to out-compete other women for the attention of men. Men pumping iron in a gym don't consider that they are trying to beat other men by looking as if they have the ability to chase and wrestle large animals and bring home the bacon. In other words, to try to look as if they can control resources.

Because of the way men's and women's criteria for their mates have evolved, it is virtually impossible for couples to co-exist without some conflict from time to time as their life circumstances change. When you accept that conflict is inevitable and you choose strategies to deal with conflicts as they occur, your life with the opposite sex can go relatively smoothly. Any thoughts you may have about conflict-free relationships are best relegated to bedtime stories or novels. The way to true relationship happiness is to understand a mate's needs and to have fulfilling those needs as your goal.

> **'Relationships are like a full-time job, and we should treat them like one. If your lover wants to leave you, they should give you two weeks' notice. There should be severance pay and a performance bonus, and before they leave, they should have to find you a temp.'**
>
> *Bob Ettinger*

Why Evolution Is Probably Over

Both the popular and scientific press love to report studies showing differences, while tending to ignore the usually more common research showing no real gender distinctions. It is all too easy to forget that men and women are far more alike than different, and that people change over time, both individually and as a society. The major cognitive gender differences have been declining significantly over the past three decades, including the 'traditional' ones of superior female verbal ability and male mathematical ability.

One of the more recent explanations for this is proposed by the theory that children are no longer segregated as far as 'male' and 'female' activities, and that behaviour has a profoundly interactive relationship with hormones and the development of cognitive skills and brain structures – for example, rough-and-tumble play, previously more common in boys, might better develop spatial abilities.

Here are four powerful tips for relationship happiness:

1 **Have a relationship coach** – a person who can see clearly what you are doing as you enter a new relationship.
2 **Don't expect a new encounter to be 'the One'.**
Statistically, it won't be. Recognise that many failed relationships can still become long-lasting friendships.
3 **Avoid the holiday trap.** Many couples falsely believe
that going on a holiday together can revive or cement a
relationship. Travelling is stressful and many relationships
come to grief on holidays because of alcohol, heightened
emotions and an unfamiliar environment. Never take a
new person to any location that brings back memories of
another experience.
4 **Avoid the baby trap.** Many couples also falsely believe
that somehow the birth of a baby will magically fix their
relationship problems. The opposite is usually the case. A
new baby becomes the centre of attention, the couple's
sex life comes to a grinding halt and their problems are
amplified. Never have a child unless your relationship is
strong and stable and a child is what you both really want.
Otherwise, unhappiness, divorce and chaos are almost
inevitable.

When to Discuss Problems

Most discussion about what we do or don't like about our sex
lives usually happens when it's present in the mind.
Unfortunately, that's usually immediately before, during or
straight after sex, which are the worst times for sex discussion,
as each person is likely to feel vulnerable. Make an appointment away from your home – at the beach, a park or coffee
lounge – with your partner to discuss your likes and dislikes.
An outside location allows each person to remain objective, as
sex is unlikely to happen at these locations (for most people).
As a woman gets older, this situation can be compounded,

as when gravity starts to take its toll on her appearance, she needs more support from a man to tell her she is still a sexy, attractive person. If she doesn't receive this support, she may begin to reject his advances. A man needs to understand that as a woman gets older, she may need more reassurance that she is still sexy and attractive to him. She needs to understand when a man wants sex he is so fuelled with testosterone he doesn't even notice wrinkles.

> **'You're a lousy lover!' she protested.**
> **'How can you tell that in four minutes?'**
> **he replied.**

Summary

The fact that much of our mate preferences and sexual urges are innate or hardwired into our brains does not necessarily condemn us to being controlled by our biology. Men are not sentenced to turbulent lives because of their need for sexual variety, and women are not doomed to spend their lives criticising men for lack of commitment. We humans differ from other animal species in that we have the ability to direct our behaviour or change it by making conscious choices. Having knowledge about why we are motivated to make the choices we do means we become accountable for our behaviour and its consequences. Having choices means that there are no more excuses for behaviour, such as 'I was so drunk I can't remember what happened' or 'I couldn't control myself' or 'Darwin made me do it!' The brain of the common moth is hardwired to allow it to navigate by the light of the moon and stars, but like humans, the moth now lives in an era that does not tolerate many of its hardwired behaviours. Today, we have insect-zappers, and if the moth blindly follows its attraction to light, it gets fried. And so will any human who refuses to acknowledge and understand the origin of our desires. We can choose to stay away from the light.

To assume that men and women are psychologically the same goes against what we know about human mating strategies and is a concept that may well be politically correct but creates confusion, unhappiness and relationship disasters for men and women everywhere. Unless men evolve into asexual beings, as some feminists would have it, men will always seek mates using youth, health and fertility as their base criteria. For their part, women will continue to seek men who have status, power and resources.

> **Understanding where we came from and how we inherited our motivations lets us control our present and direct our future.**

Some people will continue to argue that men and women now have no real differences and that, in fact, they have the same preferences and urges. That is like claiming that the weather is no longer hot or cold and that it is now always the same temperature. The reality is that the weather is the weather, regardless of how much you do or don't like it. To pretend that our sexual

> **According to the World Health Authority, 100 million acts of sexual intercourse take place every day. Right now, based on the world population:**
>
> **69,763,395 people are having sex.**
> **48,816,098 are kissing.**
> **27,250,951 are relaxing after having sex.**
> **1 poor, lonely person is reading this book.**

differences are now minimal is to pretend that men no longer grow facial hair or that women no longer develop breasts. We can only accept each other when we stop any denial or pretence about our desires, acknowledge the origins and purpose behind our impulses and develop strategies to manage those differences. This way, we can become empowered creatures of choice, rather than confused, hapless victims of our evolution.

- Discuss problems somewhere neutral at an agreed time. That way, you'll both be relaxed and more objective.
- Men and women are different. Not better, not worse, just different.
- Nevertheless, we each have the ability to make choices. By understanding our differences, we can make more informed choices for a happier future.

References

Andreasen, N. C., et al., 'Magnetic resonance imaging of the brain in schizophrenia', *Arch General Psychiatry* (1990), 47(1):35–44.

Anonymous, Sawyer, P., and Kincaid, J., *My Secret Life*, Signet Classics (2007).

Baumeister, Roy F., *Social Psychology and Human Sexuality*, Psychology Press (2001).

Becker, B., *The Player: the Autobiography*, Transworld Publishers (2005).

Becker, J. B., Breedlove, S. M., and Crews, D. (ed.), *Behavioral Endocrinology*, MIT Press/Bradford Books (1992).

Belsky, Jay, Steinberg, Laurence, and Draper, Patricia, 'Childhood experience, interpersonal development, and reproductive strategy: an evolutionary theory of socialization', *Child Development* (1991), 62:647–70.

Bergner, R. M., and Bridges, A. J., 'The significance of heavy pornography involvement for romantic partners: research and clinical implications', *Journal of Sex and Marital Therapy* (2002), 28:193–206.

Betzig, L., *Despotism and Differential Reproduction: a Darwinian View of History*, Hawthorne NY: Aldine Press (1986).

Betzig, L., 'Causes of conjugal dissolution: a cross-cultural study', *Current Anthropology* (1989), 30:654–76.

Betzig, L., 'Sex, succession and civilization in the first six civilizations' in Ellis, L. (ed.), *Social Stratification and Social Inequality*, Praeger (1993), 37–74.

Betzig, L., 'People are animals', *Human Nature: a Critical Reader*, Oxford University Press (1997), 1–13.

Black K., et al.. 'Brain morphology in eating disorders', *Biological*

Psychiatry (1990), 27:62A.

Bloom, P., 'Seduced by the Flickering Lights of the Brain', *Seed Magazine* (June/July 2006), www.seedmagazine.com/news/2006/06/seduced_by_ the_flickering_ligh.php.

Blum, D., *Sex On the Brain: the Biological Differences Between Men and Women*, Penguin (1998).

Blum, D., *Ghost Hunters: William James and the Scientific Search for Life After Death*, Penguin Press (2006).

Brewerton, T., et al., 'Eating disorders, anxiety, and 5-HT', *Biological Psychiatry* (1990), 27:41A.

Buchsbaum, M. S., 'Brain imaging in the search for biological markers in affective disorder', *Journal of Clinical Psychiatry* (1986), 47:7–12.

Buss, D. M., and Barnes, M. F., 'Preferences In Human Mate Selection', *Journal of Personality and Social Psychology* (1986), 50(3):559–70.

Buss, D. M., and Dedden, L., 'Derogation of competitors', *Journal of Social and Personal Relationships* (1990), 7:395–422.

Buss, D. M., and Schmitt, D. P., 'Sexual strategies theory: an evolutionary perspective on human mating', *Psychological Review* (1993), 100:204–32.

Buss, D. M., and Shackelford, T. K., 'From vigilance to violence: mate retention tactics in married couples', *Journal of Personality and Social Psychology* (1997), 72:346–61.

Buss, D. M., 'Sex differences in human mate preferences: evolutionary hypotheses tested in 37 cultures', *Behavioral and Brain Sciences* (1989), 12:1–49.

Buss, D. M., *The Evolution of Desire: Strategies of Human Mating*, New York, Basic Books (1994).

Buss, D. M., *Evolutionary Psychology*, Allyn & Bacon (1999).

Buss, D. M., Larsen, R. J., Westen, D., and Semmelroth, J., 'Sex differences in jealousy: evolution, physiology, and psychology', *Psychological Science* (1992), 3:251–5.

Byne, W., Bleier, R., and Houston, L., 'Variations in human corpus callosum do not predict gender', *Behavioral Neuroscience* (1988), 102(2):222–7.

Clark, R. D., and Hatfield, E., 'Gender differences in receptivity to sexual offers', *Journal of Psychology and Human Sexuality* (1989), 2:39–55.

Clarke, S., Kraftsik, R., et al., 'Forms and measures of adult and developing human corpus callosum: is there sexual dimorphism?', *J Comp Neurology* (1989), 280(2):213–30.

Cleland, J., *Fanny Hill: Memoirs of a Woman of Pleasure*, Wordsworth Editions (2001).

Corsi-Cabrera, M., Herrera, P., and Malvido, M., 'Correlation between EEG and cognitive abilities: sex differences', *International Journal of Neuroscience* (1989), 45:133–41.

Dawkins, Richard, *The Selfish Gene*, Oxford University Press (1976).

DeVries, G. J., Bruin, J. P. C., Uylings, H.B.M., and Corner, M. A. in 'Progress in Brain Research'. (1984) *The Relation Between Structure and Function*, 61. Elsevier.

Dumit, J., *Picturing Personhood: Brain Scans and Biomedical Identity*, Princeton University Press (2003), www.press.princeton. edu/titles/ 7674.html.

Ellis, B. J., and Symons, D., 'Sex differences in sexual fantasy: an evolutionary psychological approach', *Journal of Sex Research* (1990), 27:527–56.

Fisher, H., *Why We Love: the Nature and Chemistry of Romantic Love*, Henry Holt & Co. (2004).

Fontaine, R., et al., 'Temporal lobe abnormalities in panic disorder: an MRI study', *Biological Psychiatry* (1990), 27(3):304–10.

Gallagher, S., 'Predictors of SAT mathematics scores of gifted male and gifted female adolescents', *Psych. Women Quarterly* (June 1989).

Geary, D. C., 'A model for representing gender differences in the pattern of cognitive abilities', *American Psychologist* (1989).

Gottman, J. M, Murray, J. D., Swanson, C. C., Tyson, R., and Swanson, K. R., *The Mathematics of Marriage: Dynamics Nonlinear Models*, MIT Press, Bradford Books, Cambridge (2003).

Grammer, K., 'Variations on a theme: age-dependent mate selection in humans', *Behavioural and Brain Sciences* (1992), 15, 100–102 .

Grammer, K., Fink, B., Møller, A. P., and Thornhill, R., 'Darwinian aesthetics: sexual selection and the biology of beauty', *Biological Reviews* (2003), 78:385–407.

Gutek, B. A., *Sex and the Workplace: Impact of Sexual Behavior and Harassment on Women, Men and Organizations*, San Francisco: Jossey-Bass (1985).

Gutek, B. A., and Morasch, B., 'Sex ratios, sex-role spillover and sexual harassment of women at work', *Journal of Social Issues* (1982), 38(4):55–74.

Gutek, B. A., and Nakamura, C., 'Gender roles and sexuality in the world of work', *Gender Roles and Sexual Behavior*, Palo Alto, California: Mayfield (1982).

Gutek, B. A., Morasch, B., and Cohen, A. G., 'Interpreting social sexual behavior in the work settings', *Journal of Vocational Behavior* (1982), 22(1):30–48.

Gutek, B. A., Nakamura, C., Gahart, M., Handschumacher, L., and Russell, D., 'Sexuality in the workplace', *Basic and Applied Social Psychology* (1980), 1(3):255–65.

Halpern, D. F., 'The disappearance of cognitive gender differences: what you see depends on where you look', *American Psychologist* (1989).

Harvey, J. H., Wenzel, A., and Sprecher, S., *The Handbook of Sexuality in Close Relationships*, Lawrence Erlbaum (2005).

Hashimoto, T., et al., 'Magnetic resonance imaging in autism: preliminary report', *Neuropediatrics* (1989), 20(3):142–6.

Heh, C. W., 'Anxiety and anxiety disorders', unpublished paper, UC Irvine (1990).

Herholz, K., et al., 'Regional cerebral glucose metabolism in anorexia nervosa measured by positron emission tomography', *Biological Psychology* (1987), 22:43–51.

Holden, Robert, *Success Intelligence*. Hay House (2008)

Hyde, J. S., Fennema, E., and Lamon, S. J., 'Gender differences in mathematics performance: a meta-analysis', *Psych. Bulletin* (1990), 107(2):139–55.

Hyde, J. S., and Linn, M. C. (eds), *The Psychology of Gender: Advances Through Meta-Analysis* (1986).

Jankowiak, W. G., Hill, E. M., and Donovan, J. R., 'The effects of gender and sexual orientation on attractiveness judgments: an evolutionary interpretation', *Ethology and Sociobiology* (1992), 13:73–85.

Kertesz, A., 'Sex equality in intrahemispheric language organization', *Brain and Language* (1989), 37:401–8.

Kirshenbaum, M., *When Good People Have Affairs: Inside the Hearts & Minds of People in Two Relationships*, St Martin's Press (2008).

Langley, M., *Women's Infidelity – Living in Limbo: What Women Really Mean When They Say 'I'm Not Happy'*, McCarlan Publishing (2005).

Legato, M. J., and Tucker, L., *Why Men Never Remember and Women Never Forget*, Rodale Books (2006).

Luce, C. L., and Kenrick, D. T., *The Functional Mind: Readings In Evolutionary Psychology*, Allyn & Bacon (2003).

Manning, John, *The Finger Book*. Faber and Faber, (2008)

Marazziti, Donatella, *Psychological Medicine* (1999), 29:741.

Margolis, J., *O: the Intimate History of the Orgasm*, Grove Press (2005).

McCarthy, B., and McCarthy, E., *Getting It Right This Time: How to Create a Loving and Lasting Marriage*, Routledge (2005).

Michael, R. T., Gagnon, J. H., Laumann, E. O., and Kolata, G., *Sex in America*, Boston: Little, Brown (1994).

Miller, G., *The Mating Mind: How Sexual Choice Shaped the Evolution of Human Nature*, Anchor (2001).

Motley, M. T., and Reeder, H. M., 'Unwanted escalation of sexual intimacy: male and female perceptions of connotations and relational consequences of resistance messages', *Communication Monographs* (1995), 62:355–82.

Nasrallah, H. A., et al., 'A controlled magnetic resonance imaging study of corpus callosum thickness in schizophrenia', *Biological Psychiatry* (1986), 21:274.

Neuberg, S. L., Kenrick, D. T., Maner, J. K., and Schaller, M., 'From evolved motives to everyday mentation: evolution, goals, and cognition', *Social Motivation: Conscious and Unconscious Processes*, Cambridge University Press (2005).

Neuman, M. G., *The Truth About Cheating: Why Men Stray and What You Can Do to Prevent It*, Wiley (2008).

Ornish, D., *Program for Reversing Heart Disease*, Ballantine Books (2009).

Oz, M., *Healing From the Heart: a Leading Surgeon Combines Eastern and Western Traditions to Create the Medicine of the Future*, Plume (1999).

Park, J. H., and Schaller, M., 'Does attitude similarity serve as a heuristic cue for kinship? Evidence of an implicit cognitive association', *Evolution and Human Behavior* (2005), 26:158–70.

Pease, Allan, and Barbara, *Easy Peasey: People Skills for Life*, Pease International (2007).

Pease, Allan, and Barbara, *Why Men Don't Have A Clue & Women Always Need More Shoes*, Pease International (2008).

Pease, Allan, and Barbara, *Why Men Don't Listen & Women Can't Read Maps*, Pease International (2008).

Pease, Allan, and Barbara, *The Definitive Book of Body Language*, Pease International (2009).

Pease, Allan, *Questions Are the Answers*, Pease International Pty Ltd (2000).

Pease, Allan, *The Bumper Book of Rude & Politically Incorrect Jokes*, Pease International (2004).

Pease, Raymond V., *If You Won't Go Away and Leave Me Alone, I'll Find Someone Who Will!*, Pease International (2009).

Pepper, T., and Weis, D. L., 'Proceptive and rejective strategies of US and Canadian college women', *Journal of Sex Research* (1987), 23:455–80.

Pinker, Steven, *How the Mind Works*, Norton (1997).

Pollett, T. V., and Nettle, D., 'Partner wealth predicts self-reported orgasm frequency in a sample of Chinese women', *Evolution and Human Behavior* (2009), 146–51.

Quinn, Maria, *Between Clean Sheets*, HarperCollins (1994).

Reinisch, J. M., Rosenblum, L. A., and Sanders, S. A. (ed.), *Masculinity/Femininity*, Oxford University Press (1987).

Roberts, N., *Whores In History: Prostitution In Western Society*, HarperCollins (1993).

Sanders, G., and Ross-Field, L., 'Neuropsychological development of cognitive abilities', *International Journal of Neuroscience* (1987), 36:1–16.

Schaller, M., Faulkner, J., Park, J. H., Neuberg, S. L., and Kenrick, D. T., 'Impressions of danger influence impressions of people: an evolutionary perspective on individual and collective cognition', *Journal of Cultural and Evolutionary Psychology* (2004), 2:231–47.

Schneider, J. P., 'Effects of cybersex addiction on the family: results of a survey', *Sexual Addiction and Compulsivity* (2000), 7:31–58.

Shelton, R. C., et al., 'Cerebral structural pathology in schizophrenia: evidence for a selective prefrontal cort. defect', *American Journal of Psychiatry* (1988), 145:154–63.

Smith, B. D., et al., 'Hemispheric asymmetry and emotion: lateralized parietal processing of affect and cognition', *Bio. Psychology* (1987), 25:247–60.

Smith, David C., *Real-Estate Erections I Have Had*, Camel Publishing (2009).

Steele, Graham, *All the Best Ones Aren't Taken*.

Tavris, C., 'The gender gap', *Vogue* (April 1989).

Thompson, A. P., 'Extramarital relations: observations of the current situation', *Journal of Clinical Practice in Sexuality* (1987), 3(3):17, 21 and 22.

Thompson, R. A., and Nelson, C. A., 'Developmental science and the media: early brain development', *American Psychologist* (January 2001), www.content.apa.org/journals/amp/56/1/5.

Thornhill, R., and Gangestad, S. W., 'Do women have evolved adaptation for extra-pair copulation?', *Evolutionary Aesthetics* (2003).

Thornhill, R., and Grammer, K., 'The body and face of woman: one ornament that signals quality?' *Evolution and Human Behavior* (1999), 20:105–20.

Thornhill, R., and Gangestad, S. W., *The Evolutionary Biology of Human Female Sexuality*, Oxford University Press, US (2008).

Williams, G. C., *Sex and Evolution*. Princeton University Press, Princeton (1975).

Wilson, Edward Osborne, *On Human Nature*, Harvard University Press (1978).

Wright, Robert, *The Moral Animal: Evolutionary Psychology and*

Everyday Life, Pantheon Books (1994).

Wu, J., et al., 'Greater left cerebral hemispheric metabolism in bulimia assessed by positron emission tomography', *American Journal of Psychology* (1990), 147:309–12.

Zadra, A., '1093: Sex Dreams: What Do Men and Women Dream About?', *Sleep* (2007), Volume 30, Abstract Supplement, A376.

WHY MEN DON'T LISTEN
& WOMEN CAN'T READ MAPS

Have you ever wished your partner came with an instruction booklet?

Allan & Barbara Pease have spent seven years collecting research, interviewing experts and collating a comprehensive study of the profound communication differences between men and women to give us insight into why we each have a different reaction to the same thing.

In this book, the Pease's have seized upon the enormous advances made by scientists in this field. They outline how dramatic new research reveals that the wiring in male and female brains is significantly different and affects how we perceive the world and each other.

Why Men Don't Listen & Women Can't Read Maps explores this phenomenon, in the humorous style of writing that we associate with Allan & Barbara Pease.

WHY MEN DON'T HAVE A CLUE
& WOMEN ALWAYS NEED MORE SHOES!

Why are men clueless about romance, love and relationships? Why do they avoid commitment? Why do men tell lies to women and think they can get away with it?

On the other hand, why do women cry to get their own way with men and why do women insist on talking a subject to death? And why do women need more shoes instead of sex?

The gulf between the sexes, the misunderstandings and conflicts are still as present in our lives in the twenty-first century as they were when Adam first fell foul of Eve.

Let Allan & Barbara Pease, the internationally renowned experts in human relations, communication and body language, help you transform the way in which you relate to the opposite sex.

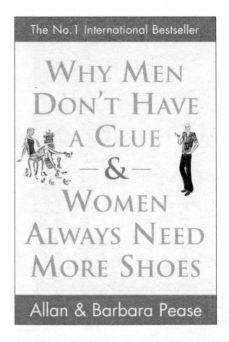

THE DEFINITIVE BOOK OF
BODY LANGUAGE

Every person's body language very often reveals that what they say is different from what they think or feel. It is a scientific fact that people's gestures give away their true intentions.

Everyday we are confronted by hundreds of different signals that can mean anything from "That's a great idea" to "You must be kidding". And we are all sending out these signals whether we realise it or not.

Body Language adds a new dimension to human communication. It is a must for anybody whose business or personal life involves face-to-face interaction with other people.

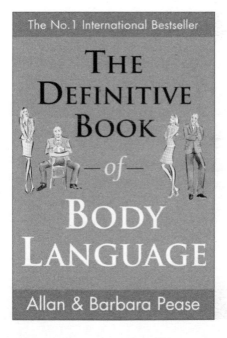

HOW TO BE A PEOPLE MAGNET
IT'S EASY PEASEY

With the right skills, motivation and a strong desire to succeed, you can accomplish anything! And who better to help you than Body Language and Communication experts, Allan & Barbara Pease.

The desire to be recognised, to feel important and appreciated is all-powerful. The more important you make someone feel, the more positively they will respond.

Communication experts, Allan & Barbara Pease present easy and effective tips to gain the right skills and motivation to succeed to accomplish anything! This programme provides you with the necessary skills to rank highly with everyone, in any situation. When you put these proven skills into action others will see you as compelling and charismatic.

This DVD and Book lets you instantly achieve extraordinary personal success. You'll find it easy to follow and easy to remember!

HOW TO DEVELOP POWERFUL COMMUNICATION SKILLS
MANAGING THE DIFFERENCES BETWEEN MEN & WOMEN

This is your survival guide for the 21st Century. It will help you dramatically improve your understanding of yourself and the opposite sex.

Men and women are different. But these differences go beyond the obvious and, if men and women are going to survive together in the modern world it is vital to develop strategies on how those differences can be addressed.

Allan & Barbara look at the evidence from recent scientific research to explain some of the deeper mysteries of men/women relationships. They answer questions that have confounded and plagued men and women for centuries.

Watch Allan Pease demonstrate how, by understanding the behaviour and needs of both sexes you can learn to get along with all your colleagues, avoid misunderstandings and arguments and help progress your career.

QUESTIONS ARE
THE ANSWERS

Top level networkers are not 'natural' or 'born'. Top level networking is a science - a learnable skill, and Questions are the Answers, gives you the techniques and shows you how to use them, how to measure and improve your progress and what to observe when dealing with people.

The Direct Marketing Business has evolved virtually overnight without fanfare or advertising and could eventually become the largest business system of them all.

It's success has been based on the referral-based distribution system and is driven almost entirely by the enthusiasm of its members. It is one of the most dynamic opportunities ever created by the mind of man, and Allan Pease has given everyone the key to unlock this system.

A 'must have' for anyone who works in sales!

EASY PEASEY
PEOPLE SKILLS FOR LIFE

With the right skills, motivation and a strong desire to succeed, you can accomplish anything! And who better to help you than Body Language and Communication experts, Allan & Barbara Pease.

Easy Peasey - People Skills for Life teaches skills that will help you to become the best person you can be, both in your professional and personal life.

The desire to be recognised, to feel important and appreciated is all-powerful. And the more important you make someone feel, the more positively they will respond to you. And that's exactly what this book will teach you!